An Analysis of

Eric Hobsbawm's

The Age of Revolution: Europe 1789–1848

Tom Stammers
with
Patrick Glen

www.macat.com
info@macat.com

Cover illustration: Etienne Gilfillan

Cataloguing in Publication Data
A catalogue record for this book is available from the British Library.
Library of Congress Cataloguing-in-Publication Data is available upon request.

ISBN 978-1-912302-63-5 (hardback)
ISBN 978-1-912127-65-8 (paperback)
ISBN978-1-912281-51-0 (e-book)

Notice

CONTENTS

THE MACAT LIBRARY

The Macat Library is a series of unique academic explorations of seminal works in the humanities and social sciences – books and papers that have had a significant and widely recognised impact on their disciplines. It has been created to serve as much more than just a summary of what lies between the covers of a great book. It illuminates and explores the influences on, ideas of, and impact of that book. Our goal is to offer a learning resource that encourages critical thinking and fosters a better, deeper understanding of important ideas.

Each publication is divided into three Sections: Influences, Ideas, and Impact. Each Section has four Modules. These explore every important facet of the work, and the responses to it.

This Section-Module structure makes a Macat Library book easy to use, but it has another important feature. Because each Macat book is written to the same format, it is possible (and encouraged!) to cross-reference multiple Macat books along the same lines of inquiry or research. This allows the reader to open up interesting interdisciplinary pathways.

To further aid your reading, lists of glossary terms and people mentioned are included at the end of this book (these are indicated by an asterisk [*] throughout) – as well as a list of works cited.

Macat has worked with the University of Cambridge to identify the elements of critical thinking and understand the ways in which six different skills combine to enable effective thinking.
Three allow us to fully understand a problem; three more give us the tools to solve it. Together, these six skills make up the **PACIER** model of critical thinking. They are:

ANALYSIS – understanding how an argument is built
EVALUATION – exploring the strengths and weaknesses of an argument
INTERPRETATION – understanding issues of meaning

CREATIVE THINKING – coming up with new ideas and fresh connections
PROBLEM-SOLVING – producing strong solutions
REASONING – creating strong arguments

To find out more, visit **WWW.MACAT.COM.**

CRITICAL THINKING AND *THE AGE OF REVOLUTION*

Primary critical thinking skill: EVALUATION
Secondary critical thinking skill: REASONING

The Age of Revolution is the first of four works by Eric Hobsbawm that collectively synthesize the ideas he developed over a lifetime spent studying the nineteenth and twentieth centuries.

Hobsbawm's vision is important – he was a lifelong Marxist whose view of history was shaped by a fascination with social and economic history, yet who privileged evidence over political theory – but the real power of these works, and especially *The Age of Revolution*, emanates from the wide range of the author's reading and his mastery of the critical thinking skill of evaluation.

It is this skill that allows Hobsbawm to combine insights drawn from decades of reading into an original thesis that sees the crucial "long 19th century" as a period shaped by "dual revolution" – the twin impacts of the Industrial Revolution in Britain, and the French Revolution on the continent. Hobsbawm supplemented his evaluative excellence with a firm grasp of reasoning, crafting a volume that contains brilliant, clearly-structured arguments which explain complicated ideas via well-chosen examples in ways that make his work accessible to intelligent general readers and scholars alike.

ABOUT THE AUTHOR OF THE ORIGINAL WORK

British historian **Eric Hobsbawm** was born in Egypt in 1917 to an
English father and Austrian mother, but the family settled in Berlin. By
1931 both of Hobsbawm's parents had died, and he and his sister were
taken in by his aunt and uncle. When the Nazis came to power in
Germany two years later, the family fled to London. Hobsbawm went to
Cambridge University, joined the British army in World War II, then
continued his academic path to become one of Britain's most respected
historians. A lifelong member of the Communist Party, Hobsbawm lived
until the grand old age of 95.

ABOUT THE AUTHORS OF THE ANALYSIS

Dr Thomas Stammers is lecturer in Modern European history at
Durham University, where he specialises in the cultural history of France
in the age of revolution. He is the author of Collection, Recollection,
Revolution: Scavenging the Past in Nineteenth-Century Paris. Dr
Stammers's research interests include a wide range of historiographical and
theoretical controversies related to eighteenth and nineteenth-century
Europe.

Dr Patrick Glen is received his doctorate from the University of
Sheffield. He currently works as a member of the faculty of the School of
Arts and Media at the University of Salford.

ABOUT MACAT

GREAT WORKS FOR CRITICAL THINKING

Macat is focused on making the ideas of the world's great thinkers
accessible and comprehensible to everybody, everywhere, in ways that
promote the development of enhanced critical thinking skills.

It works with leading academics from the world's top universities to
produce new analyses that focus on the ideas and the impact of the most
influential works ever written across a wide variety of academic disciplines.
Each of the works that sit at the heart of its growing library is an enduring
example of great thinking. But by setting them in context – and looking
at the influences that shaped their authors, as well as the responses they
provoked – Macat encourages readers to look at these classics and
game-changers with fresh eyes. Readers learn to think, engage and
challenge their ideas, rather than simply accepting them.

WAYS IN TO THE TEXT

KEY POINTS

- Eric Hobsbawm (1917–2012) was a British Marxist*
  historian, widely recognized as one of the greatest of the
  twentieth century in his field.

- *The Age of Revolution* was the first volume of Hobsbawm's
  trilogy on nineteenth-century Europe; it analyzed how the
  Industrial Revolution* in Britain and the political revolution
  in France transformed politics, society, economics and
  culture between 1789 and 1848.

- The book explores how the "dual revolution"* created
  the conditions for the growth of nineteenth-century
  capitalism* and liberalism,* first in Western Europe, and
  eventually across the globe.

Who was Eric Hobsbawm?

Eric Hobsbawm's desire to write about modern history was
powerfully shaped by his having lived in unstable times and places. He
witnessed first hand some great historical events and later wrote about
these experiences in the memoir *Interesting Times*, published in 2002.[1]

Hobsbawm was born in Alexandria, Egypt, in 1917 to Leopold
and Nelly Hobsbaum. The family later became Hobsbawm due to a
misspelling by a British consular official.[2] His parents were merchants
of Central European Jewish descent and as a youth Hobsbawm lived

in Vienna, Austria, and Berlin, Germany. But his parents had previously lived in London and spoke to Eric in English. Both of Hobsbawm's parents had died by the time he was 14 and he and his sister were taken in by relatives. The young Eric taught English to help with money. When the Nazis* came to power in Germany in 1933, his relatives fled Berlin and Eric moved to London with them. Being both Jewish and already a communist,* he would have been an obvious target for the fascist* Nazi regime.

In 1936 Hobsbawm enrolled at King's College, Cambridge* to study history and joined the Communist Party of Great Britain. During World War II* he joined the British Army, serving in the Royal Engineers and the Educational Corps. On his return to Cambridge after the war, Hobsbawm completed his PhD on the Fabian Society,* a group of late nineteenth-century socialist reformers, and then took up a lecturing post at Birkbeck,* University of London in 1947. There he founded the Communist Party Historians Group with colleagues such as E. P. Thompson,* Raphael Samuel,* George Rudé* and Dorothy Thompson.* *The Age of Revolution* was published in 1962 at a time when Hobsbawm was fully enjoying his love of jazz, hanging out at the legendary Ronnie Scott's* club in London's Soho district by night, and getting up late the following morning.

Hobsbawm continued to work on his vast survey of nineteenth- and twentieth-century world history over a number of decades. Each volume was met with huge critical praise and reached a wide readership.

Hobsbawm's reputation was such that in 2002 he became President of Birkbeck at the age of 85. He was also a fellow of the British Academy,* and had been awarded the Companion of Honour, a major title given by the British monarch for outstanding services to literature, the arts, politics, music, science, religion or industry. As British historian Tony Judt* observed, the only discrimination Hobsbawm suffered for his lifelong communism was being passed over for the chair of economic history at Cambridge. "As prices go, this would not seem particularly extortionate,"[3] he said. At the time of his death in 2012, aged 95—and despite few fellow scholars sharing his Marxist beliefs—Hobsbawm was hailed as one of the greatest historians of the post-World War II era.[4]

What Does *The Age of Revolution* Say?

In *The Age of Revolution*, Hobsbawm argues that between 1789 and 1848 two revolutions together changed the course of European history. He claims that the Industrial Revolution* in Britain and the French Revolution* that began in 1789 created the economic, political and social conditions that allowed capitalism (an economic system based on private enterprise and maximizing profit) and political liberalism (a political movement designed to encourage the freedom of the individual) to spread out from northwest Europe and transform the wider world.[5] Mixing fine detail with analysis on a grand scale, Hobsbawm explored the connections between the economic, social, political and ideological changes in this period. This set the scene for a trio of books on the "long 19th century":* After *The Age of Revolution: Europe 1789–1848* (published in 1962), came *The Age of Capital: 1848–1875* (which appeared in 1975) and *The Age of Empire: 1875–1914* (which was published in 1987).[6] All three books were seen as key works on nineteenth-century European history and were translated into 50 languages.[7] According to one reviewer, the trilogy belonged to "the mental furniture of educated Englishmen."[8]

Hobsbawm wanted to trace how the forces that created the modern world first emerged. On the one hand, the Industrial Revolution led to an explosion in the production of goods, setting free vast profits and unimaginable power. On the other hand it helped fuel new ways to exploit factory workers and others, creating bitter class conflict. In the same way, the French Revolution of 1789 had created visions of social justice and universal brotherhood. But it also led to new forms of rivalry between nations as well as some forms of political oppression, which laid the seeds for future conflict in France. Hobsbawm pointed to the double-edged nature of historical change. He saw the late-eighteenth and early-nineteenth century as not only the birthplace of capitalism, with its basis in profit and private enterprise, but also of its political opponent, socialism,* which looked to create a more just and equal society. Studying this age of revolution helped Hobsbawm to explain why Europe was the way it was at the time of the book's publication. But it also provided a promise for what Europe might become—a place where socialism might bring a fairer and more just society. Historical writing and personal political commitment always went hand in hand throughout Hobsbawm's career.

Why Does *The Age of Revolution* Matter?
The Age of Revolution argues that the changes that took place in Britain and France in the late eighteenth century went on to create the modern world. Hobsbawm clearly shows what makes the modern era different from what went before. In this sense, the book is a good case study for thinking about "periodization"—the beginnings and endings of historical eras. Hobsbawm's book runs from the 1780s, when the French king first came under attack and the British economy began to industrialize, through to the year of revolutions in 1848,* where popular uprisings against existing governments broke out in many European countries. At this point it seemed as if the newly created order—with liberal politics and a capitalist economy as its bedrock—was once again in crisis. Few could have guessed then that "what followed was not the breakdown of capitalism, but its most rapid and unchallenged period of expansion and triumph."[9]

The book is also important as a summary of Marxist views of how Western society developed in the modern era. Hobsbawm's work was admired not just in universities, but also by many left-wing thinkers and moderate politicians. Ed Miliband,* the leader of the British Labour Party,* argued after the historian's death in 2012 that

Hobsbawm "brought hundreds of years of British history to hundreds of thousands of people. He brought history out of the ivory tower and into people's lives."[10] Tony Blair,* the former Labour leader and British Prime Minister, praised Hobsbawm as a "giant of progressive politics history, someone who influenced a whole generation of political and academic leaders. He wrote history that was intellectually of the highest order but combined with a profound sense of compassion and justice. And he was a tireless agitator for a better world."[11] It could be argued that Hobsbawm's histories have above all provided an understanding of world history for the British political left. His books won him many admirers, even among those uncomfortable with his dogged defense of the communist Soviet Union.*

NOTES

1 Eric Hobsbawm, *Interesting Times: A Twentieth Century Life* (London: Allen Lane, 2002).

2 Fabrice Bensimon, "Eric Hobsbawm, 1917-2012: He Knew Everything," *Radical Philosophy* 178 (March/April 2013), 67.

3 Tony Judt, *Thinking the Twentieth Century* (London: Vintage, 2013), 62–3.

4 Niall Ferguson et al., "Eric Hobsbawm – A Historian's Historian," *Guardian*, October 1, 2012.

5 Eric Hobsbawm, *The Age of Revolution: Europe 1789–1848* (London: Abacus, 2008), 14.

6 E. J. Hobsbawm, *The Age of Capital: 1848–1875* (London: Weidenfeld & Nicolson, 1974); E. J. Hobsbawm, *The Age of Empire: 1875–1914* (London: Weidenfeld & Nicolson, 1987).

7 John Shepherd, "Eric Hobsbawm, 1917–2012," in *Labour History* 104 (2013), 221.

8 Cited in W. E. Alford, "The Age of Empire 1848–1875 by Eric Hobsbawm," in *Economic History Review* 42, no. 2 (1989), 302.

9 Hobsbawm, *Age of Revolution*, 303.

10 Esther Addley, "Eric Hobsbawm Death: Miliband Leads Tributes to 'Extraordinary' Historian," *Guardian*, October 1, 2012, 56.

11 Addley, "Eric Hobsbawm Death," 56.

SECTION 1
INFLUENCES

MODULE 1
THE AUTHOR AND THE HISTORICAL CONTEXT

KEY POINTS

- *The Age of Revolution* argues that the late eighteenth century was a key turning point in the development of modern Europe.

- Hobsbawm's lifelong support for communism* led him to study the development of capitalism* and the forces that tried to resist its advance.

- Hobsbawm's work was published at the start of the 1960s against a backdrop of socialist* revolutions and anti-colonial* movements that took place during the twentieth century.

Why Read this Text?

When he published *The Age of Revolution: Europe 1789–1848* in 1962, Eric Hobsbawm began an ambitious project: to study the "dual revolution"*—in Britain and France—that he believed transformed the world."[1] The Industrial Revolution* began by transforming Britain's economy during the 1780s. The French Revolution* of 1789 started a process that shattered the power of the monarchy and created new institutions and ideologies. Together they ushered in a world in which a rising social class, the bourgeoisie*—people who made their wealth through trade and manufacturing rather than ownership of land—could triumph. While the "dual revolution" came from Britain and France, the reforms introduced there began to spread across the continent, forming the "twin crater of a rather larger regional volcano."[2]

> **❝** The historic period which begins with the construction of the first factory system of the modern world in Lancashire and the French Revolution of 1789 ends with the construction of the first railway network and the publication of the *Communist Manifesto* **❞**
>
> Eric Hobsbawm, *The Age of Revolution*

The spread of new economic systems and new political ideas disrupted two things:

* The existing feudal* structures in the countryside, based on landowners protecting peasants in return for their work on the land.
* Absolutist* models of government, where the king or queen is the source of all authority.

The Age of Revolution is very readable, containing a wealth of useful material, and has been enjoyed by both specialist historians and interested general readers alike.

Author's Life

Hobsbawm was a committed Marxist* throughout his life and his political beliefs—that capitalism would eventually fail and be replaced by a more egalitarian* system—deeply shaped his writing of history. He had read *The Communist Manifesto,** the work of German theorists Karl Marx* and Friedrich Engels,* as a schoolboy in Germany. This experience marked not only his political views, but also his very identity. The moment *The Communist Manifesto* was published in 1848 acts as something of a climax for the story Hobsbawm outlined in *The Age of Revolution*. He said: "The historic period which begins with the construction of the first factory system of the modern world in

Lancashire and the French Revolution of 1789 ends with the construction of the first railway network and the publication of the *Communist Manifesto*."[3] He also praised Marx's major work, *Capital Volume I*, as "a marvellous, almost contemporary treatment" of the nineteenth-century economy.[4] While Hobsbawm borrowed the main outline of his interpretation of events from Marx, he also looked to enrich this framework with many examples from the real world.

Hobsbawm's communist views meant that he was passed over for the academic position of chair in economic history at Cambridge University,* but in 1947 he settled at Birkbeck,* University of London as a history lecturer. In *The Age of Revolution* Hobsbawm describes the college as a lively "alternative to the somnolence [sleepiness] of Oxford and Cambridge."[5]

During his six-decade association with Birkbeck, Hobsbawm published the installments of a four-volume survey of nineteenth and twentieth-century history. But he also wrote on many other topics too, such as the historical method (the way scholars research and write about history), international politics, and even music. (Hobsbawm originally wrote about jazz under the pseudonym Francis Newton in tribute to jazz singer Billie Holiday's* communist trumpet player.) Few writers could match Hobsbawm's variety of interests and breadth of knowledge.

Author's Background

The Age of Revolution was written at a time—1962—when another wave of revolutions was expanding across the globe. Hobsbawm was fascinated by a series of anti-colonial struggles that had developed outside Europe following the end of World War II,* as countries in Africa, Asia and the Middle East demanded—and sometimes fought long wars for—their independence from European countries. He was especially interested in the communist revolutions in China* in 1949 and Cuba* in 1959.[6] These important events showed that the era of

European empires that had been built in the nineteenth century had now proved to be only "temporary."[7] The book is optimistic about the spread of Marxist ideas around the world. Even if earlier popular uprisings had ended in failure—as in 1848*—the memory of revolution remained alive. "But if we look round the world of the 1970s," said Hobsbawm, "we shall not be tempted to underestimate the historic force of the socialist* and communist ideology born out of reaction against the dual revolution, and which by 1848 had found its first classic formulation."[8] This classic formulation—or blueprint— was provided by Marx and Engels's* *Communist Manifesto*.

Hobsbawm was a lifelong member of the Communist Party of Great Britain, and refused to leave the party—unlike several comrades such as the social historian E. P. Thompson*—when the Soviet Union* invaded Hungary in 1956.* His apparent refusal to speak out against the crimes of the U.S.S.R. (the Union of Soviet Socialist Republics, the full name of the Soviet Union, which was dissolved in 1991) invited fierce criticism from some disillusioned former Marxists such as British historian Tony Judt.* "Eric Hobsbawm is the most naturally gifted historian of our time," Judt noted in 2002; "but rested and untroubled, he has somehow slept through the terror and shame of the age."[9] After World War II ended in 1945 there was a real fear in Britain that communists were trying to gain a political foothold. Recently declassified documents show that Hobsbawm was watched by the British security services during the 1960s because of his communist sympathies.[10]

NOTES

1   Eric Hobsbawm, *The Age of Revolution: Europe 1789–1848* (London: Abacus, 2008), 11.

2   Hobsbawm, *Age of Revolution* (1962), 14

3   Hobsbawm, *Age of Revolution*, 16.

4   Hobsbawm, *Age of Revolution*, 387.

5   Hobsbawm, *Age of Revolution,* 339.

6   See essays on third-world radicals including the struggle in Vietnam, in Eric Hobsbawm, *Revolutionaries* (London: Abacus, 2007).

7   Hobsbawm, *Age of Revolution*, 40.

8   Hobsbawm, *Age of Revolution*, 16.

9   Tony Judt, "Eric Hobsbawm and the Romance of Communism," in *Reappraisals: Reflections on the Forgotten Twentieth Century* (London: Vintage, 2009), 126.

10   Richard Norton-Taylor, "MI5 spied on leading British historians for decades, secret files reveal," in *Guardian*, October 24, 2014, accessed February 26, 2015, http://www.theguardian.com/world/2014/oct/24/mi5-spied-historians-eric-hobsbawm-christopher-hill-secret-files.

MODULE 2
ACADEMIC CONTEXT

KEY POINTS

- *The Age of Revolution* reflects the post-World War* II interest in social history* — looking at the actions and ideas not only of the elites, but of the working classes too.

- The book is concerned with demonstrating that the late eighteenth century was a period of huge change and that it created the conditions for the growth of capitalism* and the power of the bourgeoisie* — the new business-owning class.

- Hobsbawm's membership of the British Communist Historians Group helped shape his thinking and turn his focus to the struggles of the working classes.

The Work In Its Context

Eric Hobsbawm had trained at Cambridge University* as an economic historian, and this shaped his ongoing interest in the history of the economic system of capitalism. Like many other scholars, he was interested in the Industrial Revolution* in Britain. Yet there was plenty of disagreement over how quickly or dramatically the Revolution came about. If economic historians were mainly concerned with how the transition to a modern economy happened, political historians wanted to explore the origins of modern political ideas such as popular sovereignty* (where the people should be the source of political authority) or representative government* (where democratically elected representatives of the people created policies for governing). Here the French Revolution* was a key turning point.

Hobsbawm wrote *The Age of Revolution: Europe 1789–1848* at a

> ❝ By any reckoning [The Industrial Revolution] was probably the most important event in world history, at any rate since the invention of agriculture and cities. And it was initiated by Britain. That this was not fortuitous is evident. ❞
>
> Eric Hobsbawm, *The Age of Revolution*

time when social history was becoming increasingly influential, and the focus shifted from writing simply the history of the elite in power to include "history from below." * In this approach, historians explored how the lower classes had created their own culture of opposition.[1] These acts of resistance were extremely important when it came to understanding the growth of nineteenth-century socialism* and the desire to reform economic and political systems to make them more fair.

Overview of the Field

A debate over how to think about the Industrial Revolution had raged ever since Cambridge University professor J. H. Clapham* helped create economic history as an academic field in its own right at the start of the twentieth century. Clapham argued that there had been a slow, uneven and delayed transition to an industrial economy. As a result, he asked whether this really deserved to be called a "revolution" at all.[2] After Clapham other scholars, including Hobsbawm, countered that there had been a dramatic "take off" in growth in the late eighteenth century as a wave of new technologies swept across the country.[3]

A heated debate was also underway before Hobsbawm over what impact industrialization had had on the working population of Britain. Hobsbawm sided with those who argued that industrialization was a disaster for the standard of living of the British working classes, many of whom were forced to move to the city to find work and found themselves living in squalor. It was the resulting misery that led to the rise of the working-class protest movement in the 1830s and 1840s known as Chartism,* with its demands for votes for all men and other democratic rights.

Political historians were also divided over the question of how much things had changed during this period. Many viewed this era as one of great instability, from the demands for the end of the French monarchy during the Revolution of 1789 to the wave of uprisings against governments right across Europe in 1848.* American historian R. R. Palmer* called it "the age of the democratic revolution."[4] Even in countries where the government was not overthrown, this was still an era of major political reform. But historians disagreed over the cause of these changes. Whig* historians in Britain—who believed in steady progress towards liberty—claimed that things were improving during this period, but added that reform had come about gradually and had been promoted by the ruling elites.[5] By contrast, Marxist* historians focused on conflict between different social groups and insisted that the authorities granted greater freedoms for the masses because of pressure from below. In France leading historians of the French Revolution, such as Georges Lefebvre,* were Marxists. They argued that 1789 was not just about a change in the way France was governed, but was in fact a "social revolution."[6] Although unsuccessful in the short-term, the French revolutionaries promoted ideas that would become central, such as politics that involved the common people and looking at making radical changes to society.

Academic Influences

After arriving in Britain from Germany in 1933 to escape the Nazis,* Hobsbawm became closely aligned with a number of intellectuals on the Left. At Cambridge he studied economic history under Michael Postan,* a pioneer of the economic history of the middle ages, who also introduced Hobsbawm to the novel methods of the Annales school* in France. This group of historians favored a broad approach to the subject, looking at culture, society, and the general population, as well as the actions of rulers. At Cambridge, Hobsbawm's interest in the history of capitalism brought him close to the Marxist economist Maurice Dobb,* while at Oxford University he had great admiration for historian G. D. H. Cole,* who had documented both the history of socialist thought and the labor movement.[7]

Hobsbawm's biggest influences, however, were his fellow members of the Communist Party Historians Group, including radical social historians such as Christopher Hill,* E. P. Thompson* and Raphael Samuel.* Hobsbawm explained that "the combination of both regular discussion and friendship was enormously stimulating and helpful and helped us to push forward our own historical development."[8] The group tried to highlight and explain the forces of oppression, exploitation and alienation* they believed the working classes suffered under.[9] They also tried to make the modern-day working classes more politically aware by providing an historical account of how their ancestors had struggled to have their own rights recognized. This struggle was fully presented in *The Age of Revolution*.

NOTES

1   For Hobsbawm's views on this development, see Eric Hobsbawm, "History from Below – Some Reflections," in *History from Below: Studies in Popular Protest and Popular Ideology*, ed. Frederick Kranz (Oxford: Oxford University Press, 1988), 13–27.

2   J. H. Clapham, *The Early Railway Age 1820–50*, vol. 2 of *An Economic History of Modern Britain* (Cambridge: Cambridge University Press, 2009).

3   T. S. Ashton, *An Economic History of England: The 18th Century* (London: Methuen, 1955).

4   R. R. Palmer, *The Age of the Democratic Revolution*, 2 vols. (Princeton: Princeton University Press, 1959–64).

5   Llewellyn Woodward, *The Age of Reform* 1815–1870 (Oxford: Oxford
    University Press, 1962).

6   Georges Lefebvre, *The Coming of the French Revolution*, trans. R. R. Palmer
    (Princeton: Princeton University Press, 1949).

7   G. D. H. Cole, *A History of Socialist Thought*, 5 vols. (London and New York:
    St Martin's Press, 1953).

8   Danny Millum, interview with Eric Hobsbawm, June 17, 2008, *History.
    ac.uk*, accessed December 2013, http:/www.history.ac.uk/makinghistory/
    resources/interviews/Hobsbawm_Eric.html.

9   For a survey of their activities, see Harvey Kaye, *The British Marxist
    Historians: an Introductory Analysis* (Cambridge: Cambridge University
    Press, 1984).

MODULE 3
THE PROBLEM

KEY POINTS

- When Eric Hobsbawm wrote *The Age of Revolution*, scholars were debating the significance of the French*— and Industrial*—Revolutions, and whether they marked a sharp break with what had come before.

- Some historians held that the changes to society had come about gradually; as a Marxist* historian, Hobsbawm tried to show that the "dual revolution"* brought radical change resulting in a new ruling class (the bourgeoisie)* and the workers' movements that opposed it.

- One of Hobsbawm's greatest achievements was to show how the two revolutions came together to create a new world order.

Core Question

Historians at the time Eric Hobsbawm was writing *The Age of Revolution: Europe 1789–1848* were concerned with the extent to which the era around 1800 saw a dramatic change in how European societies were organized. They also debated how correct the economist Karl Polanyi* was when he called this period "The Great Transformation."[1] In some ways the evidence for change was not hard to spot; the old order seemed to be shaken to its roots, with rulers toppled, religion challenged, decades of war and deep economic crisis. Yet what was the relationship, if any, between these separate changes? And if these changes were all part of a single transformation, why did it happen?

Economic historians were bitterly divided over whether the growth of industry in Britain could be characterized as a "revolution."

> ❝ Our problem is thus to explain not the existence of these new elements of a new economy and society, but their triumph; to trace not the progress of their gradual sapping and mining in previous centuries but their decisive conquest of the fortress. ❞
>
> Eric Hobsbawm, *The Age of Revolution*

Some said the term wrongly suggested a quick and unified event, while the reality was much more of a messy and drawn-out process. Political historians knew this was a period of great turmoil, especially during the explosive years of the French Revolution that began in 1789. But they did not agree on whether the turmoil could have been avoided and who was pushing the changes. Social historians focused on how the late eighteenth and early nineteenth century was the moment when mass political movements began. But how much did that, and particularly the socialist* movement, grow out of the French Revolution or the misery of industrial workers? And how close did those working-class political movements come to actually challenging the political establishment?

The Participants

Whig* historians did not accept that the events of the late eighteenth and early nineteenth century could be described as revolutionary turmoil. For them, many of the economic and political systems of the period remained, even if there were some big changes. For these historians, the radical actions of the French Revolution and the growth of socialist ideas were much less important in pushing change in Britain. These changes happened because of moderate reforms carried out by the elites who ran the country. Their careful actions were enough not just for them to hold on to power, but to make this era, according to English historian Asa Briggs,* an "age of improvement."[2] The conservative* historians did not accept the idea of sharp divisions within British society. Instead, they highlighted areas of agreement between the different social classes.

Marxist historians, by contrast, wanted to move away from a focus on the elites and instead looked to write history from below*— looking at the thoughts and actions of ordinary people. In many ways Hobsbawm was working in a similar way to E. P. Thompson,* Raphael Samuel* and George Rudé.* He spoke for all of them when he said that in the wake of the French Revolution, "What was new in the labour movement of the early nineteenth century was class consciousness and class ambition."[3] For British Marxists, the protests of those who lost out in the new industrial economy—including Luddites* (workers who destroyed the new machines that were taking away their traditional jobs), artisans and landless peasants—were a key part of the tradition that would feed into early socialism.*

In French history the Marxist approach was the most widely followed. Here, the fall of the French king was seen as the result of intense struggles between the nobility* (the rulers), the bourgeoisie (the emerging group of self-made men)* and the lower classes. Yet even here there were signs of differing views. In 1955 British historian Alfred Cobban* had already attacked the "myth" that the French bourgeoisie rebelled because they hated society under the king's rule. Cobban claimed they wanted to *join* that society and felt frustrated by the barriers blocking them. Moreover, Cobban insisted that far from helping the bourgeoisie and their new businesses, the Revolution actually set back economic growth in France for a generation.[4]

The Contemporary Debate

In exploring the remaking of society at this time, Hobsbawm relied heavily on the concepts laid out by Karl Marx* himself about the transition from "feudalism"* (where peasants worked the land in return for protection from the landowners) to "capitalism"* (where ideas of free enterprise and profit ruled).* He brought together existing research rather than exploring any new archives. But what was original about Hobsbawm's approach was bringing materials on the Industrial Revolution and the French Revolution together and thinking about the relationship between the two events.

Hobsbawm strongly believed that the late eighteenth century saw a series of unique and permanent changes. Other historians focused on examples of agreement and compromise, but he argued that the new industrial economy brought about new forms of inequality and exploitation. "The poor suffered because the rich benefitted,"[5] he wrote. In discussing the French Revolution, Hobsbawm followed French Marxist historian Georges Lefebvre* in arguing that the course of the revolution and the start of the Terror* in 1792—where terrible atrocities were carried out to "ensure" the success of the French Revolution—were explained by the clash between different social classes. He gave as examples the threat of a counterrevolution by aristocrats and the dispute between two different political factions (Girondin* and Jacobin*) over how far to support the demands of the common people. It was these arguments and disagreements that paved the way for Napoleon Bonaparte* to take advantage of the power vacuum and stage a military coup in 1799. Yet for Hobsbawm the ideals of the revolution lived on. And by placing the Industrial Revolution and French Revolution together he hoped the effects of both events would be understood more clearly.

NOTES

1   Karl Polanyi, *The Great Transformation: The Political and Economic Origins of Our Time* (Boston: Beacon Press, 2002).

2   Asa Briggs, *The Age of Improvement, 1783–1867*, vol. 8 of *A History of England*, ed. W. N. Medlicott (London: Longman, 1959).

3   Eric Hobsbawm, *The Age of Revolution: Europe 1789–1848* (London: Abacus, 2008), 254.

4   Alfred Cobban, "The Myth of the French Revolution," in *Aspects of the French Revolution* (London: Paladin, 1968), 90–111.

5   Hobsbawm, *Age of Revolution*, 254.

MODULE 4
THE AUTHOR'S CONTRIBUTION

KEY POINTS

- Eric Hobsbawm's *The Age of Revolution* has an impressively wide reach, exploring how the "dual revolution"* impacted politics, economy, culture and society.

- Hobsbawm coined the term "dual revolution" to refer to the different upheavals in France and Britain that together led to a new world order.

- Based on concepts put forward by German economist Karl Marx* more than a century earlier, the book credits the "dual revolution" with creating the bourgeoisie* and also what Marx saw as its natural enemy, the working class.

Author's Aims

Eric Hobsbawm used *The Age of Revolution: Europe 1789–1848* to explain how the French Revolution* and the British Industrial Revolution* transformed economics, politics, culture and society, laying the foundations for the modern world. Rather than treating the two major events in isolation, he argued that the revolutions in France and in Britain may have been different, but were "complementary rather than competitive."[1]

What made Hobsbawm's work remarkable was its range. While other scholars had analyzed economics, politics, social structure or culture, rarely had all these fields been brought together so skillfully within a single book. At Cambridge University* Hobsbawm had been introduced to the Annales school* of historians in France. They had inspired him with their desire for "total" history, which could include research in all disciplines and study of many different social groups.

Hobsbawm had a brilliant skill for explaining complicated things,

> ❝ The intellectual historian may (at his risk) pay no attention to economics, the economic historian to Shakespeare, but the social historian who neglects either will not get far. ❞
>
> Eric Hobsbawm, *Social History to the History of Society*

weaving together different examples into a clear and enjoyable story. He was aiming his book not just at specialists, but at "the intelligent and educated citizen, who is not merely curious about the past, but wishes to understand how and why the world has come to be what it is today and whither [where] it is going."[2] He clearly succeeded. *The Age of Revolution* was reprinted over 30 times in Britain alone and has been translated into many languages.

Approach

Hobsbawm coined the idea of a "dual revolution" to show how he believed both economic and political change had worked in parallel to overhaul "old-regime"* society—life dominated by the rule of kings and queens before the big changes. He argued that the decades from the 1780s onwards should be seen as the beginnings of the "modern" era, but this only becomes clear by thinking about politics and economics *together*. Hobsbawm pointed out that this "dual revolution" was not the result of deliberate planning. In Britain, the transition towards an economy founded around coal and cotton manufacture rose in a "rather haphazard, unplanned … way."[3] In France the Revolution was "not made or led by a formed party or movement in the modern sense, nor by men attempting to carry out a systematic programme."[4] Yet these unguided revolutions achieved results that no one could have imagined. Although after 1815 some later governments tried to turn back the clock, it was clear that the sweeping changes that had happened could not be undone.[5]

Contribution In Context

The Age of Revolution borrowed many basic ideas from the work of Karl Marx,* backing old theories with new evidence. Marx had been a great champion for extending history writing to include all sides of life and culture.[6] Both his political hopes and his writings inspired many social historians,* especially those in the British Communist Historians Group.

Marx had been an eyewitness to many of the huge industrial changes that had swept through Europe, and in his 1848 work *The Communist Manifesto** he painted a vivid picture of the bourgeoisie* coming to power and freeing new economic energies.[7] Their rise was dramatic but unstable, because the same process of industrialization that helped the bourgeoisie also created the proletariat*—or working class. According to Marx, in the end the proletariat would destroy the bourgeois moneymakers who employed them because of the terrible treatment they received at their hands. Hobsbawm adapted not just the broad outline for his book from Marx, but also many individual phrases, like the idea that capitalism* was its own "grave-digger."[8]

Hobsbawm was deeply involved in European intellectual life. He followed with great interest the attempt by Western European Marxists* to make Marx's theories fit the new challenges of the twentieth century. The bibliography for *The Age of Revolution* included writings by some of the leading socialist* scholars of the early twentieth century. Like Hobsbawm, many of them came from a Central European background. Hobsbawm's views on the relationship between the free market and state intervention mirrored those of Hungarian–American political economist Karl Polanyi.* His attention to economic cycles came from the Austrian–American economist Joseph Schumpeter.* His discussion of nineteenth-century literature was inspired by Hungarian philosopher György Lukács.* His attention to nineteenth-century science was strongly influenced by Irish fellow communist J. D. Bernal.* And his writing on how art reflected society was helped by the comments of the Hungarian Arno Hauser* and the Austrian journalist Ernest

Fischer.* In some ways *The Age of Revolution* brought together the approaches of a number of left-wing intellectuals in a range of fields.

NOTES

1   Eric Hobsbawm, *The Age of Revolution: Europe 1789–1848* (London: Abacus, 2008), 99 n. 1.

2   Hobsbawm, *Age of Revolution*, 11.

3   Hobsbawm, *Age of Revolution*, 68.

4   Hobsbawm, *Age of Revolution*, 79.

5   Hobsbawm, *Age of Revolution*, 138.

6   Karl Marx, preface to *A Contribution to the Critique of Political Economy*, trans. S. W. Ryazanskaya (Moscow: Progress Publishers, 1977).

7   Karl Marx and Friedrich Engels, *The Communist Manifesto: 150th Anniversary Edition* (London and New York: Penguin, 1998).

8   Hobsbawm, *Age of Revolution*, 297.

SECTION 2
IDEAS

MODULE 5
MAIN IDEAS

KEY POINTS

- *The Age of Revolution* shows how Britain's Industrial Revolution,* and France's political revolution, together set both economy and society on a new course.

- Against the conservative* historians who saw the "dual revolution"* as bringing about only gradual change, Hobsbawm described deep-rooted changes that had quickly favored a new class. This was the bourgeoisie* — or business owners.

- Hobsbawm aimed his book at a wide audience putting forward his view that the major changes he described promoted a working-class socialist* movement to challenge the power of the bourgeoisie.

Key Themes

Eric Hobsbawm recognized that the changes unleashed by the British Industrial Revolution of the late eighteenth century and the French Revolution* of 1789 were different, so they needed to be considered separately.

In Britain, the Industrial Revolution was not caused by superior technology, or the country having a more skilled workforce than anywhere else. Rather, it was textile production, especially cotton, control over a huge empire (India provided enormous amounts of cotton fibers) and a strong military that allowed Britain to achieve an unmatched hold over global markets. The cotton yarn and fabric was manufactured on new machine looms, powered by steam engines. This promoted the growth of factories and the cotton industry allowed rich merchants to amass huge profits, even while much of the population lived in misery. In the 1830s and 1840s those profits were

❝ Britain provided the model for railways and factories, the economic explosives which cracked open the traditional economic and social structures of the non-European world; but France made its revolutions and gave them their ideas, to the point where a tricolor [red, white and blue flag] of some kind became the emblem of virtually every emerging nation, and European (or indeed world) politics between 1789 and 1917 were largely the struggle for or against the principles of 1789, or even the more incendiary ones of 1793 [when the French king was guillotined]. **❞**

Eric Hobsbawm, *The Age of Revolution*

often invested in railways that were being built, in coal mining and the growth of heavy industry.[1]

In *The Age of Revolution: Europe 1789–1848* Hobsbawm argued that in France, meanwhile, the Revolution had an importance that went way far beyond the upheavals in other countries. This was for a number of reasons:

- It took place in the most populated and powerful kingdom in Europe.
- It was a social revolution, not just a change in the form of government.
- It aimed to spread its ideals all around the world and had an influence on uprisings as far as Latin America and India.*
- Its revolutionary government was soon pulled into a war against neighboring powers, especially Britain. That war lasted a quarter of a century and covered a quarter of the globe.
- When Britain defeated France in 1815 she removed her chief rival and so became master of the world economy.[2]

Exploring The Ideas

There are three key arguments in Hobsbawm's *The Age of Revolution*. First, he wanted to underline how this period from 1789 to 1848 created a sharp break from what went before. More conservative historians saw slow and gradual change, but Hobsbawm boldly stated that the British Industrial Revolution "forms the greatest transformation in human history since the remote times when men invented agriculture, metallurgy, writing, the city and the state."[3] The political crisis that broke out in France in 1789 was equally important, with the masses directly involved in political struggle. In the short-term the revolutionaries were not successful as the French Republic was overthrown in a military coup by Napoleon Bonaparte* in 1799. But they still handed down a powerful ideal to future generations: "the dream of equality, liberty and fraternity, and of the people rising in its majesty to shake off oppression."[4]

Second, Hobsbawm looked to show that the "dual revolution" in France and Britain created a world that was favorable to the bourgeoisie. Political signs of this included the growth of liberalism* (mainly the freedom of the individual and free trade),* limits on the powers of the church, the ending of major economic controls, and more representative governments* with the people having a say in matters of policy via elected representatives.

Careers that had previously been reserved for those of noble birth now opened up to people with talent, and a world that functioned based more on merit started to emerge. While these changes were presented as good for all citizens, they were most useful for the new bourgeois class who had the ability to get on in life.

Thirdly, this important new position of the bourgeoisie seemed very insecure. If the period from 1789 to 1848 brought new terms like "factory," "capitalist," and "liberal," it also threw up the words "socialism,"* "strike," and "pauperism."*[5] Such concepts led to the rise of the working class, who would soon begin thinking of their own interests and become a revolutionary force. The socialism that emerged in Britain and France in the 1830s and 1840s was different from previous movements that dreamt of justice or freedom. It did not look to the past, but to the future and was built on the idea of using the industrial economy for the benefit of all, rather than the profit of the few.

Language And Expression

Hobsbawm wanted to reach a broad readership with *The Age of Revolution*, and so wrote in a clear and lively way, avoiding difficult, specialist language. As a result, much of the Marxist* theory he relied on might not be immediately obvious to the reader. For instance, Marxist philosophers claimed that revolutions typically happen when there is a clash between the "means of production" (the machines and tools) and the "relations of production" (who owns them). Looking at the condition of Europe on the eve of 1848,* Hobsbawm observed that European societies were "out of balance," since the "irresistible" forces of economic, social and technical change had only produced "modest" changes in the governing institutions.[6] According to Hobsbawm, change—in the form of workers' uprisings—was sure to follow.

Hobsbawm presented a grand overview of the period, but he was not afraid to take sides. His writing about the bourgeoisie often pointed to their hypocrisy, exposing as false their claims that they had helped bring about a fair system that was open to all. The bourgeoisie introduced reforms to allow hiring based on merit and encourage people to strive for success. But the flipside of these reforms was that those who failed to prosper were judged to be morally, physically or even racially inferior.

NOTES

1   Eric Hobsbawm, *The Age of Revolution: Europe 1789–1848* (London: Abacus, 2008), 60–1, 63–4.

2   Hobsbawm, *Age of Revolution*, 124.

3   Hobsbawm, *Age of Revolution*, 13.

4   Hobsbawm, *Age of Revolution*, 98.

5   Hobsbawm, *Age of Revolution*, 13.

6   Hobsbawm, *Age of Revolution*, 366.

MODULE 6
SECONDARY IDEAS

KEY POINTS

- Although *The Age of Revolution* focuses on events in Europe, Hobsbawm connected those events to how Europe's domination of the world was slowly starting to unravel at the time he was writing.

- Hobsbawm tried to show how the "tools" of the West's control over its colonies—arms and communications—were later used by rebellious leaders against the Western colonial* powers.

- The book relates developments in Europe to events elsewhere, and helps explain how the notion of free trade*—with few restrictions placed on economic exchanges—still disadvantages poor countries today.

Other Ideas

Some recent writers have questioned Eric Hobsbawm's traditional approach to the age, often because he centered his history on Europe. The journalist and essayist David Herman* has argued, "[Hobsbawm's] books are Eurocentric. In *The Age of Revolution* there are over thirty references to Paris, twenty to Manchester but none to Boston and one to Japan. The central focus is always on the European Great Powers, and later America (which is consistently marginalized)."[1]

This criticism, however, appears less valid when *The Age of Revolution: Europe 1789–1848* is read carefully. Hobsbawm was a pioneer in writing international history. Writing at the start of the 1960s, he was very aware of living in an age of decolonization* where the British, French and Portuguese colonies in Africa, the Middle East

> ❝ The dual revolution was to make European expansion irresistible, though it was also to provide the non-European world with the conditions and equipment for its eventual counter-attack. ❞
>
> Eric Hobsbawm, *The Age of Revolution*

and Asia, gained their independence, in some cases through long wars of liberation. This was a time when a narrowly European view of world affairs was coming apart. Hobsbawm repeatedly pointed to the fact that Western domination of the world had now been shown to be "temporary."[2] Hobsbawm claimed that, "by 1848, this extraordinary future reversal of fortunes was already to some extent visible."[3] His book ends not just with Europe on the brink of the 1848 revolutions,* but also looking ahead to the first wave of resistance to imperialism* by non-European powers such as the Indian Mutiny* against the British of 1857 and the Taiping Rebellion* against the Chinese Qing dynasty in the 1850s.[4]

Exploring The Ideas

Hobsbawm said that the guns and communication tools that first allowed European states to impose their goods and values on the world in the early nineteenth century would, in time, be adopted by anti-colonial* resistance movements. This had already been seen in the attempts of Egyptian ruler Mohamed Ali* to modernize his country in the early 1800s to resist a Western advance.[5] *The Age of Revolution* identified the forces that allowed Europeans to dominate the globe, but it also showed why this control could not last. Hobsbawm showed the patterns that existed not just in the war between social classes, but also in the struggle between nations.

British and French power was all but unchallenged by the 1800s. But up until the early 1700s, "several of the great non-European powers and civilizations still confronted the white trader, sailor and soldier on apparently equal terms."[6] Hobsbawm wanted to show the tools that European states were using by the early nineteenth century to defeat their foes, creating a glaring imbalance between "the west" and "the rest," the minority against the majority of the world's inhabitants. "No fact has determined the history of the twentieth century more firmly than this."[7] Yet if Hobsbawm identified the basis of Western power, he also pointed out how these same techniques (military, administrative, technological, etc.) would over time be turned against the West by reforming rulers in the colonies.[8]

Overlooked

Despite Hobsbawm's strong links with European history, in *The Age of Revolution* he also made many comparisons between Europe and non-European societies, but these have received less critical attention. For example, he identifies the late eighteenth and early nineteenth century as a golden age for evangelical Protestantism,* which saw a new wave of missionary campaigns to far-flung regions. At the same time, there was a growth of Muslim communities in Africa, the Middle East and in Asia, amounting to what Hobsbawm called "a world Islamic revival."[9] In another example, Hobsbawm wrote about how new laws on land ownership in Europe were more harmful when "imposed on a wholly non-bourgeois* economy conquered by a bourgeois one," namely in Algeria (annexed as a colony by France in 1830).[10] Hobsbawm was sensitive to how the same reforms could have very different results when applied to different parts of the world.

Many scholars would agree with Hobsbawm that the decades around 1800 were a turning point when Britain and France strengthened their grip over their empires. The armies of the conquering French—and with them their ideas—reached into Asia and also Africa following Napoleon's* invasion of Egypt in 1798. Britain, meanwhile, as the "workshop of the world,"[11] was able to force her goods onto other nations, creating a kind of "imperialism of free trade."[12] This still remains key for understanding the relationship between trade, dependency and development even in the postcolonial* world.

NOTES

1 David Herman and E. J. Hobsbawm, "Grand Narratives and Blind Spots," *Jewish Quarterly* 59, no. 3 (2012): 18.

2 Eric Hobsbawm, *The Age of Revolution: Europe 1789–1848* (London: Abacus, 2008), 40.

3 Hobsbawm, *Age of Revolution*, 16.

4 Hobsbawm, *Age of Revolution*, 138–9.

5 Hobsbawm, *Age of Revolution*, 16.

6 Hobsbawm, *Age of Revolution*, 39.

7 Hobsbawm, *Age of Revolution*, 222.

8 Hobsbawm, *Age of Revolution*, 221.

9 Hobsbawm. *Age of Revolution*, 272–9.

10 Hobsbawm, *Age of Revolution*, 196–7.

11 Hobsbawm, *Age of Revolution*, 220.

12 Ronald Robinson, J. A. Gallagher, "The Imperialism of Free Trade," in *Economic History Review* 6, no. 1 (1953), 1–15.

MODULE 7
ACHIEVEMENT

KEY POINTS

- Hobsbawm explained how deep changes in late eighteenth-century Europe had two different results: the rise of the new factory owners and industrialists; and misery for small farmers and workers.

- Hobsbawm's book was part of a movement among historians to include the role of the workers' struggles in their writing of history.

- Hobsbawm stressed class relations, but it was at the expense of studying gender, race, and the unique ways the non-European world reacted to the changes in Europe.

Assessing The Argument

The Age of Revolution appeared in 1962 at a time when a Marxist* vision of history appeared to be gaining ground. A string of books and articles by members of the British Communist Historians Group,* including Hobsbawm, suggested that the late eighteenth and early nineteenth century were the key decades for understanding modern history. E. P. Thompson* wrote about the making of the English working class and George Rudé* explored crowd politics. They believed it was in this period that the masses became politically aware and organized for the first time. Protests, labor unions and organizations of workers at this time had long been ignored by historians. But Hobsbawm's work was part of a growing interest in social history.* This approach, following the example set by the Annales* scholars in France to use a wide variety of sources and investigate all social classes to understand events, widened the boundaries of who and what

> ❝ A new and fuller type of synthesis emerges in which such 'walls of Babylon' as those separating the two great revolutions are not only scaled but pulled down. ❞
>
> Georges Rudé, "The Age of Revolution: 1789–1848 by E .J. Hobsbawm."

historians could write about.

This interest in social history also pushed historians to notice comparisons and connections across national frontiers. *The Age of Revolution* encouraged historians in the 1960s to stop thinking about British history in isolation from developments in continental Europe. As George Rudé observed: "This newer history sees man as a social animal to be studied in relation to all his multiform activities—economic as well as political, ideological as well as social, artistic and scientific as well as military or diplomatic. Thus a new and fuller type of synthesis emerges."[3] Written at a time of socialist revolutions and decolonization* in various parts of the world, *The Age of Revolution*'s importance was clear. If the era of European and even capitalist domination seemed to be coming to an end, then it was the right time to look at how this era first began.

Achievement In Context

The first volume of *Democracy in America* owes its positive reception, in part, to the political changes taking place in France when the book was published. There were concerns about the stability of King Louis-Philippe's* regime in 1835; Tocqueville's claim that democracy was inevitable highlighted these concerns.[5]

Clearly, the book was topical. Shortly after it was published there were calls for more equality in France.[6] Its focus on the United States was of interest to French republicans who were debating whether the American model should be used in a French republic.[7]

The success of the second volume, published in 1840, was

hampered by both commercial decisions and changed political circumstances. Tocqueville initially printed the work in an expensive format, affordable only to the elite,[8] which meant that it sold more slowly than the first volume. And King Louis-Philippe's regime was more secure than it had been five years earlier. Public opinion, in other words, was no longer focused on the idea of democracy.[9] By 1848, however, there was a surge in interest in Volume Two as Louis-Philippe was overthrown and France's Second Republic* was established with Louis-Napoleon Bonaparte as president.*[10] A new publisher offered *Democracy in America* in a cheaper format, too, making it more readily available.[11]

Limitations

Like many Marxist historians of his generation, Hobsbawm's chief focus was on the relations between the social classes (e.g. factory owners, workers, peasants). He tended to neglect how the deep changes he wrote about affected women and racial minorities differently than white men. Yet later female historians like Catherine Hall* and Leonore Davidoff* went on to claim that the years around 1800 were key to the rise of a belief in "separate spheres"[4] for men and women. This was the notion that, based on both biological differences and the will of God, men should dominate the public sphere of politics, economy, commerce and law, and women, meanwhile, should inhabit the private sphere of domestic life, child-rearing, housekeeping and religious education. As industrialization started, married men left home to sell their labor for wages, whereas before they had worked around the home *alongside* their wives. Women now stayed home alone. Industrialization, therefore, helped encourage the ideology of "separate spheres." Yet as late as 1971, when Hobsbawm wrote about social history, he was silent about the particular effects of industrialization on women. It was a silence that he looked back on in 1997 with "embarrassed astonishment."[5]

Another silence concerns Hobsbawm's focus on Britain and France as the motors of historical change. Hobsbawm focused on how the innovations made in northwest Europe gradually spread to the rest of the world: "Before [i.e. Faced with] the merchants, the steam-engines, the ships and the guns of the west—and before its ideas—the age-old civilizations and empires of the world capitulated and collapsed."[6] Yet more recent scholarship has pointed to a more subtle relationship between Europe and the wider world.[7] For example, Hobsbawm mentioned the importance of markets across the empire where Britain could sell goods. This fueled the growth of cotton yarn and fabric production in Britain itself. But other scholars have stressed how the strong growth of industry in Britain actually depended on the de-industrialization—or closing of workshops—in other parts of the empire, especially India.[8] Recent research has shown that when slaves in the French colonies of Saint-Domingue and Guadeloupe rebelled in the 1790s, they did not simply follow the example of the French Republic. In fact, they went far beyond its ideas of liberty to assert new ideas of racial equality.[9] For Hobsbawm, the actions of the industrial workers were the clearest example of resistance to capitalist exploitation. But scholars looking at resistance in the colonies[10] have questioned whether this model can somehow be applied to the rural setting of a former colony like India.[11]

NOTES

1   Eric Hobsbawm, *The Age of Revolution: Europe 1789–1848* (London: Abacus, 2008), 248.

2   Hobsbawm, *Age of Revolution*, 299, 304.

3   George Rudé, "The Age of Revolution: 1789–1848 by E .J. Hobsbawm," *Science & Society* 28, no. 2 (Spring 1964): 243.

4   Catherine Hall and Leonore Davidoff, *Family Fortunes: Men and Women of the English Middle Class, 1780–1850* [1987] (London: Routledge, 2002).

5   The essay in question was "From Social History to the History of Society,"
    in Eric Hobsbawm, *On History* (London: Abacus, 1997), 71–93.

6   Hobsbawm, *Age of Revolution*, 15.

7   Maxine Berg, *Goods from the East: Trading Eurasia 1600–1800*
    (Basingstoke: Palgrave Macmillan, 2015).

8   J. R. Ward, "The Industrial Revolution and British Imperialism 1750–1850,"
    in *Economic History Review* 47, no. 1 (1994), 44–65; Clive Dewey, ed.,
    Arrested Development in India: the Historical Dimension (Delhi: Manohar
    Publications, 1988).

9   David Blackburn, *The Overthrow of Colonial Slavery, 1776–1848* (London:
    Verso Books, 2010); Laurent Dubois, *Avengers of the New World: the Story
    of the Haitian Revolution* (Cambridge MA: Harvard University Press, 2005).

10 Dipesh Chakrabarty, *Provincialising Europe: Postcolonial Thought and
    Historical Difference* (Princeton, NJ: Princeton, 2000), 11–13.

11 Ranajit Guha, *Subaltern Studies: Writings on South Asian History and
    Society* (Delhi: Oxford University Press, 1982), 1–8.

MODULE 8
PLACE IN THE AUTHOR'S WORK

KEY POINTS

- Hobsbawm wrote extensively on socialism*, industrial capitalism* and nationalism* from a Marxist* perspective; on the bicentenary of the French Revolution,* he wrote that despite the skepticism of some historians, the events of 1789 were earth shaking and changed the world for the better.

- Hobsbawm's *The Age of Revolution* was the first of his four-book series tracing 200 years of history, from the French Revolution to the collapse of the Soviet Union.*

- The book is still widely admired as elegant historical writing, even if some of its Marxist ideas may seem out of date today.

Positioning

Eric Hobsbawm's earlier books, *Labour's Turning Point* (1948)[1] and *Primitive Rebels* (1959),[2] both looked at popular movements that challenged the power of the bourgeoisie.* *Labour's Turning Point* built on the ideas of German theorist Karl Marx* and British historian G. D. H. Cole* about the working class and their political actions. In *Primitive Rebels*, though, Hobsbawm compared conservative* pre-modern social movements—the peasants in developing countries—with the early workers' movements. The topic was very timely. Hobsbawm was writing when mainly rural French and Portuguese colonies in Asia and Africa were fighting wars of independence. The theme of rural resistance comes up in *The Age of Revolution: Europe 1789–1848* too, through studies of the role of the peasantry in France

> **❝** For perhaps one of Hobsbawm's most outstanding and least commented upon achievements has been his ability to bring together the propositions of classical Marxism and the empirical preoccupations of social and economic historians into a virtually seamless web. **❞**
>
> Gareth Stedman Jones and Raphael Samuel, preface to *Culture, Ideology and Politics: Essays for Eric Hobsbawm*

in 1789 or the misery caused by the enclosure* of land in Britain at the same time. This was the dividing up of common land owned by the whole community to help develop more modern and commercial ways of farming the land.

The Age of Revolution marked a transition for Hobsbawm to writing wide-ranging works that took in events in Europe and the wider world. Although he would not often write about the late eighteenth century again, the era of the "dual revolution"* was still central to his thinking. For the 200-year anniversary of the 1789 French Revolution he wrote *Echoes of the Marseillaise*, a book that looked at how scholars' approaches toward the event had developed. Clearly troubled by rival historians who sought to play down its impact, Hobsbawm insisted the French Revolution had been a class struggle that had changed the world "for the better."[3]

Integration

With *The Age of Revolution* Hobsbawm began his vast survey of modern history. When completed it would run to four volumes: a trilogy on the "long nineteenth century"* (*Age of Revolution, Age of Capital, Age of Empire*) and then *Age of Extremes*, his account of world history from 1917 to 1991. The four books together spanned 200 years, from the French Revolution in 1789 to the collapse of the Soviet Union in 1991. Hobsbawm's real subject throughout the four books was the clash between expanding capitalism and its opponents, especially the rise and fall of socialism. It was a process that fascinated him both as a scholar and as a member of the Communist Party.

All these books reached a broad public, but Hobsbawm wrote on a huge number of other topics too. Essay collections like 1999's *Uncommon People* demonstrate his grasp of nineteenth-century labor relations as well as of modern political events like the Vietnam War* of the 1960s and 1970s and the student demonstrations in France of May 1968.* He linked these histories of resistance and rebellion to the outlaw spirit he found in his great love of jazz music.[4]

Significance

The Age of Revolution is now remembered less as a work in its own right and more as the beginning of a larger project to write the history of the "long nineteenth century." While Hobsbawm's idea of a "dual revolution" has been widely cited by others, his understanding of both the Industrial* and French Revolutions* has also been attacked. In particular some of his Marxist ideas—such as the shift from "feudalism"* to "capitalism," or the growth of "the bourgeoisie"— now seem quite dated after decades of new scholarship and the collapse of communism in Eastern Europe after the demise of the Soviet Union. *The Age of Revolution* is still admired for blending an account of events with thoughtful analysis, even if it only has an indirect influence on the agenda for research today.

Nonetheless Hobsbawm's amazing range of interest can be seen throughout his work. Like Marx before him, Hobsbawm believed in the crucial role of economics in history. But he was also very interested in the power of ideas. As he put it in a 1979 address to mark his promotion to full professor at Birkbeck,* "history can't leave out consciousness, culture and purposive [focused] action within man-made institutions."[5] Hobsbawm explored his interest in consciousness—in how people grow to feel part of a particular country or group and the power of cultural symbols—in a key work on nationalism, *The Invention of Tradition*. Published in 1983 by Hobsbawm and Terence Ranger, it was a pioneering collection of essays on "the invention of tradition." The book explored the ways in which common myths and symbols of national identity spread in a time of economic and political change.[6] Hobsbawm's later book, *Nations and Nationalism since 1780*, argued that the idea of the nation-state where politics and culture come together in a cohesive whole was not possible before the era of industrialization and mass politics.[7]

NOTES

1   E. J. Hobsbawm, *Labour's Turning Point: Extracts from Contemporary Sources* (London: Lawrence & Wishart, 1948).

2   E. J. Hobsbawm, *Primitive Rebels: Studies in Archaic Forms of Social Movement in the 19th and 20th Centuries* (London: Lawrence & Wishart, 1959).

3   Eric Hobsbawm, *Echoes of the Marseillaise: Two Centuries Look Back on the French Revolution* (London: Verso, 1990), 113.

4   Eric Hobsbawm, *Uncommon People: Resistance, Rebellion and Jazz* (London: Abacus, 1999).

5   Eric Hobsbawm, "Has History Made Progress?," in *On History* (London: Abacus, 1998), 86.

6   Eric Hobsbawm and Terence Ranger, ed., *The Invention of Tradition* (Cambridge: Cambridge University Press, 1983).

7   Eric Hobsbawm, *Nations and Nationalism since 1780: Programme, Myth, Reality* (Cambridge: Cambridge University Press, 1992).

SECTION 3
IMPACT

MODULE 9
THE FIRST RESPONSES

KEY POINTS

- *The Age of Revolution* won widespread praise, though some critics questioned its central claim that the French* and Industrial Revolutions* together were a unique, key historical development.

- Hobsbawm chose not to respond openly to his critics, although he did correct some factual errors in subsequent editions.

- The 1960s and 1970s brought new challenges to the book's claims of a sudden economic take off during the Industrial Revolution, and that sharp clashes between the social classes led to the French Revolution.

Criticism

Most critics appreciated the breadth, original thought and writing of Eric Hobsbawm's *The Age of Revolution: Europe 1789–1848.* Historian Albert Goodwin* wrote, "The work is challenging, learned, brilliant in its analytical power, wide-ranging in its lucid exposition of literary, aesthetic [artistic] and scientific achievements and packed with novel insight."[1] Professor of European history Geoffrey Bruun* complimented Hobsbawm as an "original thinker" with a distinct style and approach.[2] *The Age of Revolution* was especially admired by fellow communists, like the historian George Rudé,* who commented that the work was an "original and immensely stimulating book."[3] It praised the way in which it showed how history is an interconnected process: in Hobsbawm's hands "ideas, classes, laws and institutions cease to be static and unrelated concepts."[4]

> ❝ The French Revolution may not have been an isolated phenomenon, but it was far more fundamental than any of the other contemporary ones and its consequences were therefore far more profound. ❞
>
> Eric Hobsbawm, *The Age of Revolution*

There were, however, some minor differences over detail. As Rudé noted, this was to be expected in a book that tried to cover so much ground: "This is, of course, history on the heroic scale and any historian that operates over so wide a canvas is liable to expose himself to criticism of the narrower specialist concerned with less ambitious projects."[5] French historian Jaques Godechot* made the most blunt criticism of *The Age of Revolution*. First, he argued the book was too narrow in a geographical sense, treating Britain and France as exceptional cases and overlooking the importance of revolts elsewhere, especially Italy. Secondly, he insisted that Hobsbawm's historical analysis was weak, since the "dual revolutions"* were not really similar. In his review of the book, Godechot branded the Industrial Revolution a "picnic" compared to the French Revolution.[6] Godechot preferred a different approach that saw the French Revolution as part of series of uprisings in the late eighteenth century, including the American Revolution* between 1765 and 1783.[7]

Responses

Hobsbawm did not openly answer any of the criticism that was made of *The Age of Revolution*. In later editions, however, he did correct some of the basic errors of fact that George Rudé and Geoffrey Bruun had identified in their reviews."[8] These mistakes (such as the correct number of people guillotined along with Robespierre on June 28, 1794, or a key figure's year of birth) were sloppy, but not particularly important or controversial.

As for the attack from Godechot, Hobsbawm did not agree with viewing 1789 as simply one event in a chain of revolutions. The French Revolution was unique because it occurred in the greatest monarchy in Europe and because its ambitions and effects were universal—they spread across Europe and the world. Unlike the American Revolution,* it did not look simply to change what form of government the country should have, but was focused on a complete remaking of society. The dispute over this question was one part of the growing clash in the 1950s and 1960s between Marxist* and revisionist* historians over how to interpret the French Revolution. Both agreed that tension and conflict between the social classes was central to how the revolutions happened. The difference came in deciding whether the French Revolution was unique in its origins and its impact, and whether the bourgeoisie* was its driving force.

Conflict And Consensus

In the course of the 1960s and 1970s much more serious intellectual challenges arose. Hobsbawm based his history on a lot of research—often Marxist—that had already been published. But in the decade after his book came out, the truth or usefulness of the Marxist approach was questioned. Marxists had seen a sudden economic "take off" in the Industrial Revolution, accompanied by a dramatic shift from "feudalism"* to "capitalism."* But more and more historians began seeing a slow and uneven road leading to the new industrial economy. The economic historian Nicholas Crafts* argued that the growth of the new metal and textile industries stood alongside traditional types of manufacturing.[9] This raised doubts about the link Hobsbawm claimed between overwhelming industrialization and the beginnings of working-class political awareness.

In the field of the French Revolution, revisionist historians like Alfred Cobban,* George V. Taylor* and François Furet,* questioned the idea that separate French social classes were already at war with each other before 1789.[10] New research suggested that the bourgeoisie and the aristocracy were actually finding they had more and more in common. As a result it seemed that the Revolution might have been sparked by short-term political conflicts, rather than deeply held feelings by the bourgeoisie and the workers that they were being treated unfairly. Nor, as Hobsbawm claimed, did it seem there was evidence that 1789 had helped the growth of capitalism in France.[11] Yet Hobsbawm, described in many obituaries as stubborn, did not update the argument in light of these challenges.

NOTES

1 Albert Goodwin, "The Age of Revolution: 1789–1848 by E. J. Hobsbawm," *The English Historical Review* 79, no. 312 (1964): 617.

2 Geoffrey Bruun, "The Age of Revolution: 1789–1848 by E. J. Hobsbawm," *Political Science Quarterly* 79, no. 3 (1964): 446.

3 George Rudé, "The Age of Revolution: 1789–1848 by E. J. Hobsbawm," *Science & Society* 28, no. 2 (Spring 1964): 243.

4 Rudé, "The Age of Revolution," 244.

5 Rudé, "The Age of Revolution," 244.

6 Jaques Godechot, "The Age of Revolution, Europe from 1789 to 1848 (History of Civilisation) by E. J. Hobsbawm," *Annales historiques de la Révolution française* 36, no. 175 (1964): 109.

7 Jacques Godechot, *France and the Atlantic Revolution of the Eighteenth Century 1770–1799* (London: Macmillan, 1971).

8 Geoffrey Bruun, "The Age of Revolution: 1789–1848 by E. J. Hobsbawm," *Political Science Quarterly* 79, no. 3 (1964): 447.

9 N. F. R. Crafts, *British Economic Growth During the Industrial Revolution* (Oxford: Clarendon Press, 1986).

10 Alfred Cobban, *The Social Interpretation of the French Revolution* (Cambridge: Cambridge University Press, 1964); George V. Taylor, "Noncapitalist Wealth and the Origins of the French Revolution," in *American Historical Review* 72 (1967): 469–96; François Furet, *Interpreting*

the French Revolution, trans. Elborg Forster (Cambridge: Cambridge University Press, 1981).

11 Eric Hobsbawm, *The Age of Revolution: Europe 1789–1848* (London: Abacus, 2008), 124.

MODULE 10
THE EVOLVING DEBATE

KEY POINTS

- Hobsbawm's book is so impressive that it has been widely used by other historians, even if they question its Marxist* claim that conflict between social classes at the time of revolution was unavoidable.

- Since *The Age of Revolution* was published, many Marxist historians have moved to a more flexible understanding of social class.

- The book influenced historians to look beyond national borders and at connections between events in different countries.

Uses And Problems

Eric Hobsbawm's *The Age of Revolution: Europe 1789–1848* provided such a broad and persuasive outline that some other scholars simply adopted it and filled in missing parts of the picture. Despite the fact that Hobsbawm neglected women's history, feminist historians have found his work useful. They took his claims about the growth of industrial capitalism* to help explain the economic reasons behind the limiting of women's freedoms in the early Victorian period[1] from 1837. Men went to work, while women stayed at home. Similarly, the recent collection of essays edited by history professors Dror Wahrman* and Colin Jones* supports the idea that the late eighteenth century was indeed an "age of cultural revolutions," and that developments in Britain and France need to be studied together.[2] Hobsbawm remains an important source for all scholars who believe that the late eighteenth century was a key moment in the transition to the modern era. But

> ❝ Nothing was more inevitable in the first half of
> the nineteenth century than the appearance of labour
> and socialist movements, and indeed of mass social
> revolutionary unrest. ❞
>
> Richard Hunter, *Plato's Symposium*

many now question his belief that these changes are fully explained by
the growth of the bourgeoisie.*

Critics of Hobsbawm's Marxist view also question whether the
conflicts of the period could have been avoided, and were as
"revolutionary" as he claims. For revisionist* historians like William
Doyle,* the overthrow of the French monarchy in 1789 was not due
to long-term social conflicts, but short-term political mistakes.[3]
According to British historians like David Cannadine,* the old
landowning aristocratic families adapted to survive and kept much of
their influence despite the growing importance of industry.[4]
Historians like Linda Colley,* meanwhile, have talked about the
common loyalties that tied many British people together. Despite
belonging to different social classes, they all felt tied to the Protestant*
religion, to the nation-state, and to the expanding empire.[5] This basic
loyalty can be seen in the Chartist* movement too. Its working-class
supporters in the 1830s and 1840s demanded democratic change, but
most had little interest in revolutionary socialism.*[6] Many scholars
now question Hobsbawm's view that this was a period when instability
and conflict between social classes was unavoidable.

Schools of Thought

Many of Hobsbawm's greatest admirers shared his Leftist political
views. Eugene Genovese,* a one-time communist* historian, hailed
his work in 1984 as having "advanced a Marxism at once living,
coherent [and] undogmatic."[7] Using a Marxist approach, Hobsbawm's

books painted a rich picture that touched every part of European society.

Yet by the 1980s some of Hobsbawm's followers were saying that the idea of social classes had to be viewed more flexibly. Just because groups of workers had made demands for better conditions in the 1840s, did that mean a new social group had risen out of the Industrial Revolution?* The historian Gareth Stedman Jones* said that what happened in the early nineteenth century was not so much that new classes—the bourgeoisie and the proletariat*—came into being, but that new ways of talking about social difference appeared.[8] These "languages of class" did not only appear because of the changes in the economy, but also because of changes that were happening in the political debate. For example, there were new demands being made, like extending voting rights to wider groups of people. Stedman Jones has argued that this confusion about what social class actually means can be found throughout Marx's famous *Communist Manifesto.**[9]

From the 1980s onwards a debate started among historians about how to think about the divisions that existed in nineteenth-century society. Was it right to think of a split into two groups (the elite and the masses) or was it more about three groups: upper, middle and lower? Then again, was that society built more on a range of small differences? Perhaps one result of Hobsbawm's more flexible use of Marxist categories was to promote a shift away from seeing people's views as determined by their social class. Instead, scholars paid more attention to the role of culture and political movements in shaping what people thought.

In Current Scholarship

Hobsbawm's "dual revolution"* theory has admirers today, not just because he presented the idea so elegantly, but also because it pushed scholars to think about connections across borders. Modern historian Jan Rüger* wrote: "Eric Hobsbawm's nineteenth century remains therefore not only exemplary in the broad sweep, the elegance and style, the sheer amount of knowledge it displays; it also continues to offer a rich encouragement to think Britain and Europe in one context."[10] Today many scholars accept the importance of producing histories of the revolutionary era in Britain and France that, if not comparative, at least explore connections between, the two countries. For example, intellectual historians look at how thinkers from different backgrounds exchanged ideas on economics or republicanism. Social historians look at how artisans became involved in political fights. Political historians look at military mobilization in an age of war. And cultural historians look at wider communications between England and France.[11]

Most scholars today, however, do not share Hobsbawm's Marxist belief in the rise to power of the bourgeoisie. History professor Sarah Maza* has further adapted the argument of Gareth Stedman Jones to go so far as to claim that the bourgeoisie never really existed as a group. She believes the term was used as a negative label to describe certain types of self-advancing behavior.[12] This shift in the 1980s away from looking at class relations to looking at culture as a way to understand history worried Hobsbawm. He was convinced that Karl Marx* had truly asked the most fundamental questions about social change and still agreed with his belief that conflicts between social classes moved history forwards.[13]

NOTES

1 Judith Newton et al, ed., *Sex and Class in Women's History* (London: Routledge and Kegan Paul, 1983).

2 Colin Jones and Dror Wahrman, ed., *The Age of Cultural Revolutions: Britain and France 1750–1820* (Berkeley: University of California Press, 2002).

3 William Doyle, *Origins of the French Revolution* (Oxford: Oxford University Press, 1980).

4 David Cannadine, *The Decline and Fall of the British Aristocracy* (London: Picador, 1992).

5 Linda Colley, *Britons: Forging the Nation, 1707–1832* (New Haven: Yale University Press, 1992); Kathleen Wilson, *The Island Race: Englishness, Empire and Gender in the Eighteenth Century* (London: Routledge, 2002); John Parry, *The Politics of Patriotism; English Liberalism, National Identity and Europe 1830–1886* (Cambridge: Cambridge University Press, 2006).

6 Malcolm Chase, *Chartism: A New History* (Manchester: Manchester University Press, 2007).

7 Eugene Genovese, "The politics of class struggle in the history of society: an appraisal of the work of Eric Hobsbawm," in *The Power of the Past: Essays for Eric Hobsbawm*, ed. Pat Thane et al. (Cambridge: Cambridge University Press, 1984), 13.

8 Gareth Stedman Jones, *Languages of Class: Studies in English Working-Class History 1832–1982* (Cambridge: Cambridge University Press, 1984).

9 Gareth Stedman Jones, Introduction to *The Communist Manifesto: 150th Anniversary Edition* (London and New York: Penguin, 1998), 27–38, 177–84.

10 Jan Rüger, "Britain, Empire, Europe: Re-reading Eric Hobsbawm," *Journal of Modern European History* 11 (2013), 421.

11 Emma Rothschild, *Economic Sentiments: Adam Smith, Condorcet, and the Enlightenment* (Cambridge MA: Harvard University Press, 2001); Rachel Hammersley, *French Revolutionaries and English Republicans: the Cordeliers Club 1790–94* (London: Boydell Press, 2011); David Bell, *The First Total War: Napoleon's Europe and the Birth of Modern Warfare* (London: Bloomsbury, 2008); Iorwerth Prothero, *Radical Artisans in England and France 1830–70* (Cambridge: Cambridge University Press, 1997); Renaud Morieux, *Une mer pour deux royaumes: La Manche, frontière franco-anglaise* (XVII–XVIIIe) (Rennes: Presses universitaires de Rennes, 2008).

12 Sarah Maza, *The Myth of the French Bourgeoisie: An Essay on the Social Imaginary 1750–1850* (Cambridge MA: Harvard University Press, 2005).

13 Eric Hobsbawm, "Marx and History" in *On History* (London: Abacus, 1998), 207–25.

MODULE 11
IMPACT AND INFLUENCE TODAY

KEY POINTS

- *The Age of Revolution* appears widely on undergraduate reading lists as a very important work, even if there are question marks over some of its fine detail.

- The book contains some crude Marxist* ideas. But the fact that it takes in such a wide range of political, economic, social and cultural information was a big breakthrough at the time after previous histories focused on the actions of the ruling elites.

- Hobsbawm has inspired debates on a number of the key points he wrote about, including the expansion of industry and the beginnings of liberalism.*

Position

Eric Hobsbawm's *The Age of Revolution: Europe 1789–1848* is a widely respected introduction to European history and to the events of the time that went on to transform the world. The text shows considerable skill in combining a wide range of source materials and has a secure place on undergraduate reading lists. Commenting on Hobsbawm's work, modern history lecturer David Priestland* said, "At a time when academic historians were becoming increasingly suspicious of 'grand narratives', he saw how important it was to understand the broader forces of historical change."[1]

In recent years other textbooks covering this whole period have been published, such as Tim Blanning's* *The Pursuit of Glory*, Robert Gildea's* *Barricades and Borders* or Jonathan Sperber's* *Revolutionary Europe 1780–1880*.[2] These works are not Marxist, and class struggle is

> **❝** The movements of economies, ideologies and states were not always synchronous [happening at the same time]. They tended to be interactive. The French Revolution, the dominant political event of the period, occurred before significant industrialization had occurred even in Britain, and few historians now see the revolution as a triumph of the 'bourgeoisie' **❞**
>
> C. A. Bayly, *The Birth of the Modern World, 1780–1914*

only one part of their stories. However, as their titles suggest, these works tend to go along with Hobsbawm's view that a deep transformation did occur as the eighteenth century moved into the nineteenth. They disagree with Hobsbawm, though, in their chronologies (when exactly did the continent's "old regime"* disappear? 1799? 1815? 1848?); in their geography (what about the situation in Central, Eastern and Southern Europe?) and above all in their approach to the bourgeoisie.* Hobsbawm saw the bourgeoisie as the "new, rational men of ability rather than birth"[3] who swept away the old order. In a very provocative book American historian Arno Mayer* argues that the old European nobles were not removed at all, but held on to power all the way through to the outbreak of World War I*, showing "the persistence of the old regime."[4]

Interaction

Hobsbawm argued with confidence that the Industrial Revolution* happened as a sudden economic "take off" from the 1780s onwards. But new research has made the picture more complex.[5] For example a boom in consumption during the eighteenth century appears to have been a key factor driving the growth in manufacturing.[6] In economic terms, this suggests the importance not only of the supply of new goods—but also of the demand for them—in the expansion of the new industrial economy. Other historians have focused on Britain's success in spreading new skills and technology in making her Europe's "first knowledge economy."[7] Such scholars would adjust Hobsbawm's dates by placing the first sparks of the Industrial Revolution a hundred years earlier during the Enlightenment* of the late seventeenth century. Other historians, meanwhile, claim it took far longer than Hobsbawm suggests for the effects of the "dual revolution"* to be fully felt. Historian Richard N. Price* says that many of the changes Hobsbawm claimed for the early nineteenth century actually only became visible more than half a century later, in the 1880s and 1890s.[8]

Yet while his economic explanations might now seem crude, Hobsbawm made one of the few serious attempts to write a Marxist history of the modern world—a project that has had many imitators on the Left.[9] International histories produced in Britain after World War II* focused mainly on diplomacy and the roles of kings and prime ministers. But Hobsbawm wrote a new kind of history that took in economics, society, and culture.[10] He had a big impact on the historians of the long nineteenth century,* who followed. C.A. Bayly,* author of *The Birth of the Modern World, 1789–1914*, disagreed with parts of Hobsbawm's approach, especially his focus on the bourgeoisie. But Bayly praised Hobsbawm's trilogy[11] as the "most powerfully written and consistent of all the English-language world histories in print."[12]

The Continuing Debate

Cambridge University* historian C.A. Bayly is one of many admirers of Hobsbawm who disagree with some of his conclusions. For example, Bayly agrees that the "desire of capitalists to maximize their income and to subordinate labor was an inexorable [unstoppable] force for change, not just in the west, but across Asia and Africa."[13] But he says this mentality did not really take hold until the 1840s and 1850s. Hobsbawm, Bayly claims, was wrong to see it as closely connected to political events in France in the 1790s.[14]

Hobsbawm's work has encouraged debate on the major changes that took place in the nineteenth century. Political and economic liberalism—and the individual freedoms it promotes—are widely seen as having played a big role in the developments of the early part of that century. Liberalism became, in Professor Frank Trentmann's* words, a "secular gospel."[15] In exploring the explosion of free trade,* another Cambridge historian, Boyd Hilton,* saw connections between evangelical Protestantism* and the rise of laissez-faire economics* where major restrictions on the development of an economy were to all intents and purposes removed. These religious evangelists wanted free trade to flourish without interference because they saw this as clearing a pathway for God to work his will as he saw fit.[16] Hobsbawm may have exaggerated the importance of radicalism and early socialism* in nineteenth century Britain, but he was right to suggest it spread fear among the ruling classes. This made liberalism, the opposite of socialism, more attractive to the elites.

NOTES

1   Niall Ferguson et al., "Eric Hobsbawm– A Historian's Historian," *Guardian,* October 1, 2012.

2   Tim Blanning, *The Pursuit of Glory: Europe 1648–1815* (London: Penguin, 2008); Robert Gildea, *Barricades and Borders: Europe 1800–1914* (Oxford: Oxford University Press, 1996); Jonathan Sperber, *Revolutionary Europe, 1780–1850* (London: Routledge, 2000).

3   Eric Hobsbawm, *The Age of Revolution: Europe 1789–1848* (London: Abacus, 2008), 22.

4   Arno J. Mayer, *The Persistence of the Old Regime: Europe to the Great War* (London: Croom Helm, 1981).

5   Maxine Berg and Pat Hudson, "Rehabilitating the Industrial Revolution," *Economic Historical Review* 45, no. 1 (1992): 24–50.

6   Jan de Vries, *The Industrious Revolution: Consumer Behaviour and the Household Economy, 1650 to the Present* (Cambridge: Cambridge University Press, 2008); Neil McKendrick et al, ed., *The Birth of a Consumer Society: The Commercialization of Eighteenth-Century England* (Bloomington:

University of Indiana Press, 1985); Maxine Berg, *Luxury and Pleasure in Eighteenth-Century Britain* (Oxford: Oxford University Press, 2005).

7   Joel Mokyr, *The Enlightened Economy: Britain and the Industrial Revolution 1700–1850* (London: Penguin, 2011); Margaret Jacob, *The First Knowledge Economy: Human Capital and the European Economy, 1750–1850* (Cambridge: Cambridge University Press, 2014).

8   Richard Price, *British Society 1680–1880: Dynamism, Containment and Change* (Cambridge: Cambridge University Press, 1999).

9   For a polemical modern treatment, see Chris Harman, *A People's History of the World: From the Stone Age to the New Millennium* (London: Verso, 2008); Domenico Losurdo, *Liberalism: A Counter-History*, trans. Gregory Elliot (London: Verso, 2014).

10 For sophisticated examples of international history in the 1950s, see A. J. P. Taylor, *The Struggle for Mastery in Europe, 1848–1918* (Oxford: Clarendon Press, 1954); Lewis Namier, *Vanished Supremacies: Essays on European History 1812–1918* (London: Hugo Hamilton, 1958).

11 Alongside *The Age of Revolution*, Hobsbawm also wrote *The Age of Capital: 1848–1875* and *The Age of Empire: 1875–1914*.

12 C. A. Bayly, *The Birth of the Modern World 1780–1914* (London: Blackwell, 2004), 5.

13 Bayly, *Birth of the Modern World*, 5.

14 Bayly, *Birth of the Modern World*, 5–7.

15 Frank Trentmann, *Free Trade Nation: Commerce, Consumption and Civil Society in Modern Britain* (Oxford: Oxford University Press, 2009).

16 Boyd Hilton, *The Age of Atonement: The Influence of Evangelicalism on Social and Economic Thought 1795–1865* (Oxford: Clarendon Press, 1997).

MODULE 12
WHERE NEXT?

KEY POINTS

- Hobsbawm never renounced his Marxist* approach to history, but towards the end of his life he did call for a new radical politics to replace the failed communist* model.

- Since *The Age of Revolution* the fashion in history writing has shifted from discussing revolution and social change to looking at meaning and identity. But the 2008 financial crisis has given rise to new works exploring the true nature of capitalism.*

- *The Age of Revolution* introduced lots of ordinary people to "the long nineteenth century,"* and it remains one of the best examples of a Marxist approach to history.

Potential

The international popularity of Eric Hobsbawm's *The Age of Revolution: Europe 1789–1848* means that it will remain an influential work of popular history for students and interested readers all over the world. In a clear and elegant way it argues that the French Revolution* and the Industrial Revolution* together made the bourgeoisie* masters both at home and abroad in the early nineteenth century. The work shows the value of a comparative approach to history (especially across borders) and this approach has been widely imitated in the current fashion for "transnational history."* The study of the French Revolution, for example, has broadened in recent years to include discussion of events in North America, Latin America and the Caribbean.[1] As French specialist Annie Jourdan* has put it, 1789 can no longer be seen as "l'exception française,"[2] or the French exception.

> **❝** Such a way of working has not so much been an application of Marxism, as a new form of it, the creation of a new type of Marxist history, which simply did not exist before. **❞**
>
> Gareth Stedman Jones and Raphael Samuel, preface to *Culture, Ideology and Politics: Essays for Eric Hobsbawm*

After the failure of Marxism in the Soviet Union* and information on the horrors of leader Joseph Stalin's* rule became available,[3] the international Left lost a lot of support. Many of Hobsbawm's friends and fellow historians—including E. P. Thompson*—moved away from the Communist Party to commit themselves to other left-wing causes. Hobsbawm's continued loyalty to the party and to a Marxist analysis of history might now seem dated. *The Age of Revolution* confidently points to socialism* as "the child of capitalism" and a tool that can resist capitalism's excesses in exploiting people. But socialism has been in retreat in Western Europe for much of the past 30 years. Yet rather than give up his old beliefs, Hobsbawm tried to adapt them to the new times.[4] By 2009 he was calling for a new form of progressive radical politics to stand up both to communism's failure and to capitalism's "bankruptcy."[5]

Future Directions

The Age of Revolution only has an indirect influence on the academic debate today. The type of Marxism and "history from below"* that Hobsbawm proposed seems quite a traditional approach compared to newer methods that have followed on from poststructuralism* and the cultural turn,* where undisputed interpretations are seen as unreliable.[6] To generalize, radical historians still practice "history from below," but the focus has changed these days from looking at overall revolution and social change to delving into meaning, representations and identity. A good example would be Emma Griffin's* study of the Industrial Revolution through the memoirs of hundreds of men and women. While Griffin's work does show some of the new opportunities for social mobility created by the new industrial economy, the focus is primarily on how individuals experienced and found their way through those changes.[7]

Throughout his life, Hobsbawm remained committed to writing broad accounts that explored how politics, economics, social relations, and culture together shaped history. This has been an inspiration for scholars like David Armitage* and William Sewell* who worry that the study of history today is being broken down into focused areas that are too small.[8] The financial crisis in 2008 has stimulated a new wave of writing about the development of capitalism, with important works by the geographer David Harvey,* the economist Thomas Piketty* and the anthropologist David Graeber.* But rather than simply repeat the classic Marxist positions, each has borrowed Marxist tools to come up with better understandings of how capitalism operates and how it shapes history.[9] *The Age of Revolution* is still one important way of understanding the changes that created our modern world.

Summary

The Age of Revolution has shaped how generations of students think about the "dual revolution,"* how it transformed the world and then began to create modern society, economics and culture. According to Hobsbawm, the Industrial Revolution in Britain and the political revolution in France interacted with one another. Together they created capitalist* and liberal* regimes that were friendly to a new class, the bourgeoisie. This change freed vast new productive forces, but it also created "the ugliest world in which man had ever lived."[10] As a result, this world generated conflicts that would bring its mortal enemy—socialism—much closer. Karl Marx* saw this pattern where opposing forces clash and something new emerges (a dialectic* pattern) as the motor pushing history forward. Hobsbawm explores this idea fully in *The Age of Revolution*, which remains an ideal introduction to the transformations in Britain and France of the period.

Hobsbawm was a key British historian, and a leading twentieth-century intellectual. His Marxist beliefs have lost support since the failure of the Soviet Union,* but his passion and genius for history has won compliments from all sides. *The Age of Revolution* has introduced many people to the "long nineteenth century," and that in itself makes it a valuable historic work.

NOTES

1   Lynn Hunt et al, ed., *The French Revolution in Global Perspective* (Ithaca, NY: Cornell University Press, 2013).

2   Annie Jourdan, *La Révolution: une exception française?* (Paris: Flammarion, 2006).

3   Joseph Stalin (1878–1953) led the Soviet Union from 1924 to 1953, and was responsible for the deaths of millions through political purges, Terror and coercive economic policies.

4   Eric Hobsbawm, *Globalization, Democracy and Terrorism* (London: Abacus, 2008).

5   Eric Hobsbawm, "Socialism has Failed. Now Capitalism is Bankrupt. So What Comes Next?" *Guardian*, April 10, 2009, 46.

6   Lynn Hunt and Victoria Bonnell, ed., *Beyond the Cultural Turn: New Directions in the Study of Society and Culture* (Berkeley: University of California Press, 1999).

7   Emma Griffin, *Liberty's Dawn: A People's History of the Industrial Revolution* (New Haven: Yale University Press, 2014).

8   William Sewell, *Logics of History: Social Theory and Social Transformation* (Chicago: University of Chicago Press, 2005).

9   David Harvey, *The Enigma of Capital: And the Crises of Capitalism* (New York: Profile Books, 2011); Thomas Piketty, *Capital in the Twenty-First Century*, trans. Arthur Goldhammer (Cambridge MA: Harvard University Press, 2013); David Graeber, *Debt, the First 5000 Years* (New York: Melville House, 2013).

10 Eric Hobsbawm, *The Age of Revolution: Europe 1789–1848* (London: Abacus, 2008), 360.

GLOSSARY

GLOSSARY OF TERMS

1848 Revolutions: "the year of revolutions," with uprisings against existing governments breaking out across Europe. Britain, Belgium and Russia were the only exceptions.

1968 Protests: May 1968 saw huge demonstrations in France by an alliance of students and labor unions against the government of the day. That year also saw many other protests around the world, often to show anger at American foreign policy in the Vietnam War and to make demands for greater personal and sexual freedoms.

Absolutism: mode of governance that emerged in the monarchies of seventeenth- and eighteenth-century Europe, stressing the sovereign as the source of all authority.

Alienation: word adopted by Karl Marx, specifically referring to a condition of workers in a capitalist economy that comes from being unable to identify with the products of their labor and from a sense of being controlled or exploited.

American Revolution: uprising by the 13 North American colonies against the British government, which led to the American War of Independence (1775–83) and the creation of the United States.

Annales school: twentieth-century French school of the study of history, associated with Lucien Febvre, Marc Bloch and Fernand Braudel. It was noted for its commitment to innovative and interdisciplinary methods of study.

Anti-colonial struggles: violent and non-violent struggles adopted by many countries in Africa, Asia and the Middle East that had been colonized by several European powers including Great Britain and France.

Birkbeck: part of the University of London where Eric Hobsbawm spent the majority of his career.

Bourgeoisie: term coined in medieval France that came to loosely refer to urban groups who made their wealth through trade or services, rather than from ownership of land. Karl Marx used the term more specifically to identify the class of property owners who had taken power from the old aristocracy and made vast fortunes out of capitalism by exploiting the working classes.

British Academy: national academy in Britain that funds and provides support for the arts and humanities.

Cambridge University: A public research university founded in 1209 in Cambridge, England. Alongside Oxford University, it is one of the two oldest educational institutions in Britain; together they are widely considered to be among the world's best universities.

Capitalism: economic system based on private ownership, private enterprise and the maximization of profit.

Chartism: British working-class movement of the 1830s and 1840s aimed at achieving electoral reform, including the right to vote for all adult men of sound mind.

Chinese Communist Revolution: 1949 revolution that saw the Chinese Communist Party under Mao Zedong overthrow the Nationalist government and create a one-party state.

Colonialism: the rule of the native population by people from another territory.

Communism: ideology that aims at the abolition of private property, an end to capitalism and the creation of an equal society.

The Communist Manifesto: an 1848 political pamphlet by German philosophers Karl Marx and Friedrich Engels that laid out the ideas of the international political party the Communist League.

Conservatism: political belief system that sees human nature as individualistic and guided by self-interest. This approach favors the survival of established institutions and the maintenance of traditional authority and norms.

Cuban Communist Revolution: 1959 revolution led by Fidel Castro's 26th July Movement that deposed the government of Fulgencio Batista.

The Cultural Turn: idea that swept across the humanities in the 1980s and 1990s. Under the influence of French philosophical ideas, all-encompassing narratives fell out of favor as historians paid more attention to questions of meaning, representation and subjectivity.

Decolonization: the process by which territories which once belonged to European empires gained independence. The process happened at different points in the years following the end of World War II.

Dialectic: a way of thinking first developed by Georg Hegel and then adapted by Karl Marx claiming that all phenomena develop through contradiction. Opposing forces clash and out of this conflict new combinations emerge, leading to a constant process of destruction and creation.

Dual revolution: expression coined by Eric Hobsbawm to describe the Industrial Revolution in Britain and the French Revolution of 1789. Although different, Hobsbawm believed they interacted to produce radical transformations of European society.

Egalitarianism: the belief that all humans are equal.

Enclosure: the policy of dividing up "commons"—lands that were traditionally held by the whole community—to spread more commercial agriculture. Enclosure acts began in the sixteenth century, but accelerated from the late eighteenth century.

Enlightenment: a movement of late seventeenth- and eighteenth-century Europe that emphasized the use of reason to increase knowledge and improve society.

Fabian Society: left-wing group founded in Britain in 1884 that advocated evolutionary rather than revolutionary socialism. Its members included Sidney and Beatrice Webb and George Bernard Shaw.

Feudalism: economic and social system associated with medieval Europe based on the relationships between landowners and laboring tenants. Military protection is offered by landowners in return for agricultural work from tenants.

Free trade: an ideology that believes there should be minimal or no restrictions or tariffs placed on economic exchange.

French Revolution: term used to describe the political upheaval that began in France in 1789 and lasted for a decade, leading to a dramatic period of reform, the proclamation of the French Republic in 1792, and the violence of the Terror.

Girondin: French political group of committed republicans during the French Revolution. They were wary of sacrificing their principles to appeal to the popular masses.

History from below: phrase sometimes attributed to Georges Lefebvre or Lucien Febvre, "history from below" ("*histoire d'en bas*") seeks to view history from the perspective not just of the rulers, but also the ruled.

Hungarian Uprising: 1956 revolt by the Hungarian people against their Soviet-controlled government. The uprising was violently suppressed.

Imperialism: policy of extending a country's power or influence abroad through diplomacy or military force.

Indian Mutiny: failed uprising against British rule in India in 1857. Referred to in India as the first war of independence.

Industrial Revolution: period of enormous industrial and economic growth that began in Britain around 1760 and eventually spread to many other European states. It was driven by advances in mechanical technology that harnessed steam and water power to mass-produce goods, starting with textiles.

Jacobin: a French group—also known as The Society of the Friends of the Constitution—that emerged during the French Revolution and provided the support-base for radical politicians. Jacobins demonstrated flexibility in their principles and were willing to do anything to help safeguard the Republic.

Labour Party: Founded in 1893 and the main center-left party in the United Kingdom, in opposition to the center-right Conservative Party.

Laissez-faire economics: term to describe a policy that favors little governmental economic control or intervention.

Liberalism: a political movement associated with maximizing the freedom of the individual, free trade and moderate, continuous reform. Hobsbawm argued that liberalism emerged in the era of the French Revolution.

Long nineteenth century: term referring to the period from 1789 to 1914, i.e. from the French Revolution to the outbreak of World War I. It was a way of "periodizing" history, popularized by Hobsbawm.

Luddites: group of early nineteenth-century workers who tried to destroy the machines that threatened to abolish their traditional livelihood.

Marxism: political group profoundly influenced by the writings and methods of German philosopher Karl Marx. Marxists believe that capitalism will inevitably be destroyed and be replaced with a more equal communist system.

Nationalism: a feeling of pride for one's country that often goes hand in hand with a sense of superiority over other countries.

Nazi: extreme right-wing political party that ruled Germany between 1933 and 1945. The Nazis (short for National Socialists) were led by Adolf Hitler.

Old regime: feudal social and political order established in the Kingdom of France from approximately the fifteenth century to the late eighteenth century.

Pauperism: general term for being poor, but also a specific English usage term for people who were entitled to some sort of state help when finding themselves in great financial difficulty.

Popular sovereignty: idea asserting that it is the people who are and should be the source of all political authority in a state. This was a chief principle asserted in France in 1789.

Postcolonial: referring to the period following colonial rule.

Poststructuralism: literary and philosophical movement that emerged in France in the 1970s. Poststructuralism seeks to critique the search to find stable meanings, emphasizing instead a number of different viewpoints and interpretations and less emphasis on finding definitive meanings.

Proletariat: term used by Karl Marx to denote the industrial working classes exploited by capitalism and with nothing to lose from revolution. Marx believed that the proletariat would lead a future communist revolution.

Protestantism: strand of Christianity that emerged during the Reformation. It denies the authority of the Pope and places emphasis on Biblical truth and a personalized faith. Anglicans, Lutherans, Methodists and Baptists are all Protestant denominations.

Representative government: idea demanding that citizens have the right to participate in the forming of government policy, often through electing representatives to express their views.

Revisionist historians: historians who question and revise previously accepted positions.

Social history: broad branch of history that studies the experiences of ordinary people as opposed to focusing on officials and other powerful people.

Socialism: political movement, believed by Eric Hobsbawm to have been first created in the early nineteenth century, seeking to reform capitalism to create a more just and equal society. Marxism is one of many variants of socialism.

Soviet Union: communist state (1922–91) based on principles of Marxist-Leninism (trying to implement communism via a dictatorship). Encompassed Russia and its surrounding states in Eastern Europe and Central Asia.

Taiping Rebellion: huge, religiously-inspired rebellion (1850–64) against the Qing dynasty in China. The rulers survived thanks to assistance from Britain and France.

The Terror: brutal period in French history between 1792 and 1794 that emerged in parallel with the establishment of the French Republic. Involved the ruthless elimination of presumed enemies of the state.

Transnational history: approach to interlinking history encouraged in the 2000s as a way of exploring phenomena that cross the borders of nation-states.

Vietnam War: war waged by the United States in Southeast Asia from 1964 until 1975 in a failed attempt to prevent the nationalist and communist north from reuniting the country with the south.

Whig History:A view of history that believes in steady progress towards liberty and enlightenment characterized by constitutional government, individual freedoms and scientific improvement.

World War I: an international conflict between 1914 and 1918 centered in Europe and involving the major economic world powers of the day.

World War II: Global conflict between 1939 and 1945 that pitted the Axis Powers of Nazi Germany, Fascist Italy and Imperial Japan against the Allied nations including Britain, the USA and the USSR.

PEOPLE MENTIONED IN THE TEXT

Mohamed Ali (1769–1849) rebelled against the Ottoman Empire to become self-proclaimed ruler of Egypt and Sudan, introducing a host of modernizing reforms in his country.

David Armitage (b. 1965) is a British historian based at Harvard University who has worked on the history of imperialism and constitution making. In the 2014 History Manifesto he urged his fellow historians to return to "big questions."

Christopher Bayly (b. 1945) is a professor emeritus in Indian and global history at the University of Cambridge. He has produced his own global account of the "long nineteenth century."

John Desmond Bernal (1901–71) was a scientist best known for his work on X–ray crystallography and molecular biology, but also for his writings on the history of science and communist belief.

Tony Blair (b. 1953) is a former leader of the Labour Party (1994–2007) and British Prime Minister (1997–2007). An architect of "New Labour," he steered the party away from its socialist past.

T. C. W. Blanning (b. 1942) is professor of European history at Cambridge University. He has published widely on the French revolutionary wars, the cultural politics of the eighteenth century and the history of music.

Asa Briggs (b. 1921) is an English historian based at Sussex famed for his important work on Victorian culture, Chartism and broadcasting. His survey of nineteenth-century politics was entitled *The Age of Improvement: 1783–1867* (1959).

Geoffrey Bruun (1898–1988) was a professor of French, European, and American History at New York University.

David Cannadine (b. 1950) is a professor at Princeton University and a celebrated historian of the British aristocracy, imperial culture and class.

John H. Clapham (1873–1946) was the first professor of economic history at the University of Cambridge and provost of King's College, Cambridge, as well as the author of important works on the Industrial Revolution and the Bank of England.

Alfred Cobban (1901–68) was a British historian of France, based at the University of London. Cobban began the wave of revisionism that questioned the accuracy of the Marxist understanding of 1789.

George Douglas H. Cole (1889–1959) was a British historian, economist, jurist and political theorist at Oxford University. He researched socialism and co-operative movements.

Linda Colley (b. 1949) is professor at Princeton and an authority on questions of British national and imperial identity in the eighteenth century.

Nicholas Crafts (b. 1949) is professor of British economic history at the University of Warwick. He has argued influentially for the slow spread and growth of the Industrial Revolution in Britain.

Leonore Davidoff (1932–2014) was a historian and sociologist at Essex University famed for her studies of nineteenth-century class, gender and family relationships.

Maurice Dobb (1900–76) was an economist based at Cambridge University who was crucial in spreading Marxist ideas among his students. His important works include *Studies in the Development of Capitalism* (1946).

William Doyle (b. 1942) is professor of history at Bristol and a leading revisionist interpreter of the French Revolution. He has published classic survey works and recent studies on the European aristocracy.

Friedrich Engels (1820–83) was an influential German philosopher, social scientist, and political theorist who worked closely with Karl Marx.

Ernst Fischer (1899–1972) was a key figure in the Austrian Communist Party who published on cultural topics including *The Necessity of Art* (1959).

François Furet (1927–97) was a former Marxist who, disillusioned with Soviet communism, abandoned social explanations in the 1970s to become the most important French historian of the Revolution through his emphasis on politics, culture and discourse.

Eugene Genovese (1930–2012) was the foremost Marxist historian of slavery in the American south, using Marxist methods to understand slave rebellion and resistance. He later moved away from left-wing politics.

Robert Gildea (b. 1952) is professor of history at Oxford University. He has published widely on French political traditions, May 1968 and the French Resistance.

Jacques Godechot (1907–89) was a French historian, influenced by Marxism and the Annales, and a pioneer of Atlantic history.

Albert Goodwin (1906–85) was a professor of modern history at the University of Oxford and an expert on revolutionary France.

David Graeber (b. 1961) is an American anthropologist and political activist based at the London School of Economics. He has produced critical work on the history of debt and lent support to the Occupy Wall Street movement.

Emma Griffin is a history professor at the University of East Anglia specializing in working class life during the Industrial Revolution.

Catherine Hall (b. 1946) is professor of history at University of London and a pioneer of feminist history and the history of the British Empire.

David Harvey (b. 1935) is professor in geography and anthropology at City University of New York, famed for his radical, Marxist approach to the study of urban development.

Arnold Hauser (1892–1978) was a Hungarian art historian who adopted a Marxist approach to art history, claiming to find a link between the developments of naturalistic and realist art and the growth of the bourgeoisie.

Georg Wilhelm Friedrich Hegel (1770–1831) was a German idealist philosopher who exerted an enormous influence on Karl Marx, and claimed that human history was the progressive unfolding of spirit or consciousness.

David Herman is a contemporary journalist and essayist.

Christopher Hill (1912–2003) was a British Marxist historian based at Oxford University. He pioneered social history approaches to the study of popular culture and belief in the seventeenth century.

Boyd Hilton (b. 1944) is professor of British history at Cambridge University. He is the widely acclaimed author of works on the links between evangelical religion and political economy.

Billie Holiday (1915–59) was an African–American jazz singer. She was much admired by Hobsbawm.

Colin Jones (b. 1947) is professor of history at Queen Mary College at the University of London and is a much-published cultural historian of France.

Annie Jourdan is associate professor of European studies at the University of Amsterdam, and has published on monuments and political culture during the French Revolution and Napoleonic Wars. She champions the use of comparative perspectives when studying the period.

Tony Judt (1948–2010) was a British historian, essayist and intellectual who specialized in twentieth-century European history.

Georges Lefebvre (1874–1959) was the leading historian of the French Revolution who created the outlines of the Marxist interpretation of 1789 and was famed for his remarkable archival work on the peasantry. He was the author of *The Coming of the French Revolution* (1939).

György Lukács (1885–1971) was a Hungarian philosopher and literary critic who, after serving briefly in Hungary's communist government of 1919, dedicated himself to writing about nineteenth-century European literature.

Karl Marx (1818–83) was a German economist, historian, philosopher, and social theorist whose conception of history and economic writings provided the ideological basis for communism.

Sarah Maza (b. 1953) is professor of history at Northwestern University and has published widely on legal culture in France from the eighteenth to the twentieth centuries.

Arno J. Mayer (b. 1926) is a professor at Princeton University. He has published widely on nineteenth-century Europe, the Holocaust and revolutionary violence.

Ed Miliband (b. 1969) is a British Labour politician and the current leader of the Labour Party. His father Ralph Miliband was an associate of Hobsbawm in British communist circles.

Napoleon Bonaparte (1769–1821) was born in Corsica and rose spectacularly through the French army to become general. In 1799 he overthrew the French Republic in a coup d'état and in 1804 declared himself Emperor. His military and political genius made him master of Europe until his defeat to the British at Waterloo in 1815.

Robert Roswell Palmer (1909–2002) was an American historian based at Princeton whose most famous work was the two-volume *Age of the Democratic Revolution* (1959–64).

Thomas Piketty (b. 1971) is professor of economics at EHESS in Paris. He has achieved worldwide recognition for his work *Capital* (2013), based on years of research related to inequality and wealth distribution.

Karl Polanyi (1886–1964) was a Hungarian–American political economist famed for his work *The Great Transformation* (1944) on the changing relationship between the market and the state in the aftermath of the Industrial Revolution.

Sir Michael Moissey Postan (1899–1981) was a prominent British economic historian who researched medieval economic history.

Richard N. Price is professor of British history at the University of Maryland and an advocate for the slow evolution of nineteenth-century economy and society. He has recently explored Victorian governance of Africa.

David Priestland is a lecturer in modern history at Oxford University who specializes in communist regimes and broad political history.

Jean-Jacques Rousseau (1712–78) was a Swiss philosopher, novelist and composer famed for his critique of commercial society and his political theory of the social contract.

George Rudé (1910–93) was a British Marxist historian who did pioneering work on crowds and politics in the French Revolution and in Britain in the age of reform.

Jan Rüger is reader in modern history at Birkbeck and an authority on the industrial competition between Britain and Germany in the nineteenth century.

Raphael Samuel (1934–96) was a British Marxist historian who researched working-class and labor history. He wrote a number of well-respected books on British identity, people's history and communism.

Joseph Schumpeter (1883–1950) was a Czech-born Austrian–American economist, who wrote widely on economic cycles and produced the classic work *Capitalism, Socialism, Democracy* (1942).

Ronnie Scott (1927–96) was a British jazz musician and club proprietor.

Jonathan Sperber (b. 1952) is professor of history at the University of Missouri. He is an acclaimed historian of nineteenth-century Europe, especially focusing on the 1848 revolutions and the career of Karl Marx.

Joseph Stalin (1878–1953) led the Soviet Union from 1924 to 1953 and was responsible for the deaths of millions through political purges and coercive economic policies.

Gareth Stedman Jones (b. 1942) is professor of the history of ideas at Queen Mary University of London. He made crucial contributions to the history of the British working classes and the politics of the

New Left before turning to intellectual history and the study of political economy.

George V. Taylor (1919–2011) was an American historian based at Chapel Hill in North Carolina who wrote a series of landmark articles on the French eighteenth-century economy in the 1960s.

Dorothy Thompson (1923–2011) was a British Marxist historian who researched Chartism, gender history and Irish history.

E. P. Thompson (1924–93) was the foremost British social historian of the latter half of the twentieth century. A passionate Marxist, he wrote the seminal *The Making of the English Working Classes* (1963). Unlike Hobsbawm he left the Communist Party after the Hungarian uprising of 1956.

Frank Trentmann is professor of history at Birkbeck and specializes in modern British economic history and the history of consumption.

Dror Wahrman is professor of British history at the University of Indiana and the Hebrew University in Jerusalem, famed for his works on middle-class identity and on selfhood in the eighteenth century.

Beatrice Potter Webb (1858–1943) was an English social reformer who co-founded the London School of Economics and Political Science, and the Fabian Society She wrote widely on the history of trade unionism and women's issues.

Sidney Webb (1859–1947) was a British socialist, economist and historian, who belonged to the Fabian Society and was a co-founder of the London School of Economics and Political Science.

WORKS CITED

WORKS CITED

Addley, Esther. "Eric Hobsbawm Death: Miliband Leads Tributes to 'Extraordinary' Historian." *Guardian*, October 1, 2012.

Alford, W. E. "The Age of Empire 1848–1875 by Eric Hobsbawm." *Economic History Review* 42, no. 2 (1989): 302–3.

Ashton, T. S. *An Economic History of England: The 18th Century*. London: Methuen & Co., 1955.

Bayly, C. A. *The Birth of the Modern World 1780–1914*. London: Blackwell, 2004.

Imperial Meridian: The British Empire and the World, 1780–1830. London: Longman, 1989.

Bell, David A. *The First Total War: Napoleon's Europe and the Birth of Modern Warfare*. London: Bloomsbury, 2008.

Bensimon, Fabrice. "Eric Hobsbawm, 1917–2012: He Knew Everything." *Radical Philosophy* 178 (March/April 2013).

Berg, Maxine. *Goods from the East: Trading Eurasia 1600–1800*. Basingstoke: Palgrave Macmillan, 2015.

Luxury and Pleasure in Eighteenth-Century Britain. Oxford: Oxford University Press, 2005.

Maxine, and Pat Hudson. "Rehabilitating the Industrial Revolution." *Economic Historical Review* 45, no. 1 (1992): 24–50.

Blackburn, Robin. *The Overthrow of Colonial Slavery, 1776–1848*. London: Verso Books, 2011.

Blanning, Tim. *The Pursuit of Glory: Europe 1648–1815*. London: Penguin, 2008.

Briggs, Asa. *The Age of Improvement, 1783–1867*. Vol. 8 of *A History of England*, edited by W. N. Medlicott. London: Longman, 1959.

Bruun, Geoffrey. "The Age of Revolution: 1789–1848 by E. J. Hobsbawm." *Political Science Quarterly* 79, no. 3 (1964): 446–7.

The Decline and Fall of the British Aristocracy. London: Picador, 1992.

Chakrabarty, Dipesh. "Minority Histories, Subaltern Past." *Postcolonial Studies* 1, no. 1 (1998): 15–29.

Provincialising Europe: Postcolonial Thought and Historical Difference. Princeton, NJ: Princeton University Press, 2000.

Macat Analysis of **Eric Hobsbawm's** *The Age of Revolution*

Chase, Malcom. *Chartism: A New History*. Manchester: Manchester University Press, 2007.

Clapham, J. H. *The Early Railway Age 1820–50*. Vol 1 of *An Economic History of Modern Britain.* Cambridge: Cambridge University Press, 2009.

Cobban, Alfred. "The Myth of the French Revolution." [1955] In *Aspects of the French Revolution*. London: Paladin, 1968.

The Social Interpretation of the French Revolution. Cambridge: Cambridge University Press, 1964.

Cohen, G. A. *Karl Marx's Theory of History: A Defence*. Princeton: Princeton University Press, 1978.

Cole, G. D. H. *A History of Socialist Thought*. 5 vols. London and New York: St Martin's Press, 1953.

Colley, Linda. *Britons: Forging the Nation, 1707–1832*. New Haven: Yale University Press, 1992.

Crafts, N. F. R. *British Economic Growth during the Industrial Revolution*. Oxford: Clarendon Press, 1986.

De Vries, Jan. *The Industrious Revolution: Consumer Behaviour and the Household Economy, 1650 to the Present*. Cambridge: Cambridge University Press, 2008.

Dewey, Clive, ed. *Arrested Development in India: the Historical Dimension*. Delhi: Manohar Publications, 1988.

Doyle, William. *Origins of the French Revolution*. Oxford: Oxford University Press, 1980.

Dubois, Laurent. *Avengers of the New World: the Story of the Haitian Revolution*. Cambridge MA: Harvard University Press, 2005.

Ferguson, Niall, et al. "Eric Hobsbawm – A Historian's Historian." *Guardian,* October 1, 2012.

Furet, François. *Interpreting the French Revolution.* Translated by Elborg Forster. Cambridge: Cambridge University Press, 1981.

Genovese, Eugene. "The politics of class struggle in the history of society: an appraisal of the work of Eric Hobsbawm." In *The Power of the Past: Essays for Eric Hobsbawm*, edited by Pat Thane, Geoffrey Crossick, and Roderick Floud, 13–36. Cambridge: Cambridge University Press, 1984.

Gildea, Robert. *Barricades and Borders: Europe 1800–1914*. Oxford: Oxford University Press, 1996.

Godechot, Jaques. "The Age of Revolution, Europe from 1789 to 1848 (History of Civilisation) by E. J. Hobsbawm." *Annales historiques de la Révolution française* 36, no. 175 (1964): 108–11.

France and the Atlantic Revolution of the Eighteenth Century 1770–1799.
London: Macmillan, 1971.

Goodwin, Albert. "The Age of Revolution: 1789–1848 by E. J. Hobsbawm." *The English Historical Review* 79, no. 312 (1964): 616–17.

Graeber, David. *Debt, the First 5000 Years*. New York: Melville House, 2013.

Griffin, Emma. *Liberty's Dawn: A People's History of the Industrial Revolution.*
New Haven: Yale University Press, 2014.

Guha, Ranajit. *Subaltern Studies: Writings on South Asian History and Society.*
Delhi: Oxford University Press, 1982.

Hall, Catherine, and Leonore Davidoff. *Family Fortunes: Men and Women of the English Middle Class, 1780–1850* . London: Routledge, 2002.

Hammersley, Rachel. *French Revolutionaries and English Republicans: the Cordeliers Club 1790–94*. London: Boydell Press, 2011.

Harman, Chris. *A People's History of the World: From the Stone Age to the New Millennium*. London: Verso, 2008.

Harvey, David. *The Enigma of Capital: And the Crises of Capitalism*. New York:
Profile Books, 2011.

Herman, David, and E. J. Hobsbawm. "Grand Narratives and Blind Spots."
Jewish Quaterly 59, no. 3 (2012): 16–21.

Hilton, Boyd. *The Age of Atonement: The Influence of Evangelicalism on Social and Economic Thought 1795–1865*. Oxford: Clarendon Press, 1997.

A Mad, Bad, and Dangerous People? England 1783–1846. Oxford: Oxford University Press, 2006.

Hobsbawm, E. J. *The Age of Capital: 1848–1875*. London: Weidenfeld & Nicolson, 1975.

The Age of Empire: 1875–1914. London: Weidenfeld & Nicolson, 1987.

The Age of Extremes: The Short Twentieth Century 1914–1991. London: Michael Joseph, 1994.

The Age of Revolution: Europe, 1789–1848. London: Abacus, 2008.

Bandits. London: Weidenfeld & Nicolson, 1969.

Echoes of the Marseillaise: Two Centuries Look Back on the French Revolution.
London: Verso, 1990.

"From Social History to the History of the Social." In *On History*. London:

Abacus, 1998.

Globalization, Democracy and Terrorism. London: Abacus, 2008.

"Has History Made Progress?" In *On History*. London: Abacus, 1998.

"History from Below – Some Reflections." In *History From Below: Studies in Popular Protest and Popular Ideology*, edited by Frederick Kranz, 13–27. Oxford: Oxford University Press, 1988.

Interesting Times: A Twentieth Century Life. London: Allen Lane, 2002.

Labour's Turning Point: Extracts from Contemporary Sources. London: Lawrence & Wishart, 1948.

"Marx and History." In *On History*. London: Abacus, 1998.

Nations and Nationalism since 1780: Programme, Myth, Reality. Cambridge: Cambridge University Press, 1992.

"Postmodernism in the Forest." In *On History*. London: Abacus, 1998.

Primitive Rebels: Studies in Archaic Forms of Social Movement in the 19th and 20th Centuries. London: Lawrence & Wishart, 1959.

Revolutionaries. London: Abacus, 2007.

"Socialism has Failed. Now Capitalism is Bankrupt. So What Comes Next?" *Guardian*, April 10, 2009.

Uncommon People: Resistance, Rebellion and Jazz. London: Abacus, 1999.

Hobsbawm, E. J. [Francis Newton, pseud.]. *The Jazz Scene*. London: Weidenfeld & Nicolson, 1959.

Hobsbawm, E. J., and George Rudé. *Captain Swing*. London: Weidenfeld & Nicolson, 1969.

Hobsbawm, E. J., and T. O. Ranger, eds. *The Invention of Tradition: Further Studies in the History of Labour*. Cambridge: Cambridge University Press, 1983.

Howe, Steven. *Empire: A Very Short Introduction*. Oxford: Oxford University Press, 2002.

Hunt, Lynn, and Victoria Bonnell, eds. *Beyond the Cultural Turn: New Directions in the Study of Society and Culture*. Berkeley: University of California Press, 1999.

Hunt, Lynn, Suzanne Desan and William Nelson, eds. *The French Revolution in Global Perspective*. Ithaca, NY: Cornell University Press, 2013.

Jacob, Margaret. *The First Knowledge Economy: Human Capital and the*

European Economy, 1750–1850. Cambridge: Cambridge University Press, 2014.

John, Maya. "Remembering Eric Hobsbawm and his Age: A Journey from Popular Front to New Labour." *Social Scientist* 40, no. 11 (2012): 89–100.

Jones, Colin, and Dror Wahrman, eds. *The Age of Cultural Revolutions: Britain and France 1750–1820*. Berkeley: University of California Press, 2002.

Jourdan, Annie. *La Révolution: une exception française?* Paris: Flammarion, 2006.

Joyce, Patrick. "The End of Social History." *Social History* 20 (1995): 73–91.

Judt, Tony. "Eric Hobsbawm and the Romance of Communism." In *Reappraisals: Reflections on the Forgotten Twentieth Century*. London: Vintage, 2009.

Thinking the Twentieth Century. London: Vintage, 2013.

Kaye, Harvey. *The British Marxist Historians: an Introductory Analysis*. Cambridge: Polity Press, 1984.

Kettle, Martin, and Dorothy Wedderburn. "Eric Hobsbawm Obituary." *Guardian*, October 1, 2012.

Laity, Paul. "The Great Persuader." *Guardian*, September 1, 2007.

Lefebvre, Georges. *The Coming of the French Revolution*. Translated by R. R. Palmer. Princeton: Princeton University Press, 1949.

Lenin, V.I. *Imperialism, the Highest Stage of Capitalism*. London: International Publishers, 1969.

Losurdo, Domenico. *Liberalism: A Counter-History*. Translated by Gregory Elliot. London: Verso, 2014.

Mandler, Peter. *Aristocratic Government in the Age of Reform: Whigs and Liberals 1830–1852*. Oxford: Oxford University Press, 1990.

Marx, Karl. Preface to *A Contribution to the Critique of Political Economy*. Translated by S. W. Ryazanskaya. Moscow: Progress Publishers, 1977.

Marx, Karl, and Friedrich Engels. *The Communist Manifesto: 150th Anniversary Edition*. London and New York: Penguin, 1998.

Mayer, Arno J. *The Persistence of the Old Regime: Europe to the Great War*. London: Croom Helm, 1981.

Mayfield, David, and Susan Thorne. "Social history and its discontents: Gareth Stedman Jones and the Politics of Language." *Social History* 17 (1992): 165–88.

Maza, Sarah. *The Myth of the French Bourgeoisie: An Essay on the Social*

Imaginary 1750–1850. Cambridge MA: Harvard University Press, 2005.

McKendrick, Neil, J. H. Plumb and John Brewer, eds. *The Birth of a Consumer Society: The Commercialization of Eighteenth-Century England*. Bloomington: University of Indiana Press, 1985.

Mokyr, Joel. *The Enlightened Economy: Britain and the Industrial Revolution 1700–1850*. London: Penguin, 2011.

Morieux, Renaud. *Une mer pour deux royaumes: La Manche, frontière franco-anglaise* (XVIIe–XVIIIe siècles). Rennes: Presses universitaires de Rennes, 2008.

Namier, Lewis. *Vanished Supremacies: Essays on European History 1812–1918*. London: Hugo Hamilton, 1958.

Newton, Judith, Mary Ryan and Judith Walkowitz, eds. *Sex and Class in Women's History*. London: Routledge and Kegan Paul, 1983.

Norton-Taylor, Richard. "MI5 spied on leading British historians for decades, secret files reveal." *Guardian*, October 24, 2014.

Ostelhammel, Jürgen. *The Transformation of the World: A Global History of the Nineteenth Century*. Princeton: Princeton University Press, 2014.

Palmer, R. R. *The Age of the Democratic Revolution*. 2 vols. Princeton: Princeton University Press, 1959–64.

Parry, John. *The Politics of Patriotism: English Liberalism, National Identity and Europe 1830–1886*. Cambridge: Cambridge University Press, 2006.

Piketty, Thomas. *Capital in the Twenty-First Century.* Translated by Arthur Goldhammer. Cambridge MA: Harvard University Press, 2014.

Polanyi, Karl. *The Great Transformation: The Political and Economic Origins of Our Time*. Boston: Beacon Press, 2002.

Price, Richard. *British Society, 1680–1880: Dynamism, Containment and Change*. Cambridge: Cambridge University Press, 1999.

Prothero, Iorwerth. *Radical Artisans in England and France 1830–1870*. Cambridge: Cambridge University Press, 1997.

Robinson, Ronald, and J. A. Gallagher. "The Imperialism of Free Trade." *Economic History Review* 6, no. 1 (1953): 1–15.

Rothschild, Emma. *Economic Sentiments: Adam Smith, Condorcet, and the Enlightenment*. Cambridge MA: Harvard University Press, 2001.

Rudé, George. "The Age of Revolution: 1789–1848 by E.J. Hobsbawm." *Science & Society* 28, no. 2 (Spring 1964): 242–5.

Rüger, Jan. "Britain, Empire, Europe: Re-reading Eric Hobsbawm." *Journal of Modern European History* 11 (2013): 417–23.

Sewell, William. *Logics of History: Social Theory and Social Transformation*. Chicago: University of Chicago Press, 2005.

Shepherd, John. "Eric Hobsbawm, 1917–2012." *Labour History* 104 (2013): 221–4.

Shovlin, John. *The Political Economy of Virtue: Luxury, Patriotism and the Origins of the French Revolution*. Ithaca NY: Cornell University Press, 2007.

Sperber, Jonathan. *Revolutionary Europe, 1780–1850*. London: Routledge, 2000.

Stedman Jones, Gareth. *Languages of Class: Studies in English Working Class History 1832–1982*. Cambridge: Cambridge University Press, 1984.

Stedman Jones, Gareth, and Raphael Samuel, eds. *Culture, Ideology and Politics: Essays for Eric Hobsbawm*. London: Routledge & Kegan Paul, 1982.

Taylor, A. J. P.*The Struggle for Mastery in Europe, 1848–1918*. Oxford: Clarendon Press, 1954.

Taylor, George V. "Noncapitalist Wealth and the Origins of the French Revolution." *American Historical Review* 72 (1967): 469–96.

Thane, Pat, and Geoffrey Crossick. "Introduction. Capitalism and the pre-capitalist heritage." In *The Power of the Past: Essays for Eric Hobsbawm*, edited by Pat Thane, Geoffrey Crossick and Roderick Floud, 1–11. (Cambridge: Cambridge University Press, 1984).

Thompson, E. P. *The Making of the English Working Class*. London: Penguin, 1980.

Trentmann, Frank. *Free Trade Nation: Commerce, Consumption and Civil Society in Modern Britain*. Oxford: Oxford University Press, 2009.

Ward, J. R. "The Industrial Revolution and British Imperialism 1750–1850." *Ec*Wilson, Kathleen. *The Island Race: Englishness, Empire and Gender in the Eighteenth Century*. London: Routledge, 2002.

Winch, Donald. *Riches and Poverty: An Intellectual History of Political Economy in Britain 1750–1834*. Cambridge: Cambridge University Press, 1996.

Woloch, Isser. *The New Regime: Transformations of the French Civic Order, 1789–1820s*. New York: Norton, 1995.

Woodward, Llewellyn. *The Age of Reform, 1815–1870*. Oxford: Clarendon Press, 1962.

THE MACAT LIBRARY
BY DISCIPLINE

AFRICANA STUDIES

Chinua Achebe's *An Image of Africa: Racism in Conrad's Heart of Darkness*
W. E. B. Du Bois's *The Souls of Black Folk*
Zora Neale Huston's *Characteristics of Negro Expression*
Martin Luther King Jr's *Why We Can't Wait*
Toni Morrison's *Playing in the Dark: Whiteness in the American Literary Imagination*

ANTHROPOLOGY

Arjun Appadurai's *Modernity at Large: Cultural Dimensions of Globalisation*
Philippe Ariès's *Centuries of Childhood*
Franz Boas's *Race, Language and Culture*
Kim Chan & Renée Mauborgne's *Blue Ocean Strategy*
Jared Diamond's *Guns, Germs & Steel: the Fate of Human Societies*
Jared Diamond's *Collapse: How Societies Choose to Fail or Survive*
E. E. Evans-Pritchard's *Witchcraft, Oracles and Magic Among the Azande*
James Ferguson's *The Anti-Politics Machine*
Clifford Geertz's *The Interpretation of Cultures*
David Graeber's *Debt: the First 5000 Years*
Karen Ho's *Liquidated: An Ethnography of Wall Street*
Geert Hofstede's *Culture's Consequences: Comparing Values, Behaviors, Institutes and Organizations across Nations*
Claude Lévi-Strauss's *Structural Anthropology*
Jay Macleod's *Ain't No Makin' It: Aspirations and Attainment in a Low-Income Neighborhood*
Saba Mahmood's *The Politics of Piety: The Islamic Revival and the Feminist Subjec*t
Marcel Mauss's *The Gift*

BUSINESS

Jean Lave & Etienne Wenger's *Situated Learning*
Theodore Levitt's *Marketing Myopia*
Burton G. Malkiel's *A Random Walk Down Wall Street*
Douglas McGregor's *The Human Side of Enterprise*
Michael Porter's *Competitive Strategy: Creating and Sustaining Superior Performance*
John Kotter's *Leading Change*
C. K. Prahalad & Gary Hamel's *The Core Competence of the Corporation*

CRIMINOLOGY

Michelle Alexander's *The New Jim Crow: Mass Incarceration in the Age of Colorblindness*
Michael R. Gottfredson & Travis Hirschi's *A General Theory of Crime*
Richard Herrnstein & Charles A. Murray's *The Bell Curve: Intelligence and Class Structure in American Life*
Elizabeth Loftus's *Eyewitness Testimony*
Jay Macleod's *Ain't No Makin' It: Aspirations and Attainment in a Low-Income Neighborhood*
Philip Zimbardo's *The Lucifer Effect*

ECONOMICS

Janet Abu-Lughod's *Before European Hegemony*
Ha-Joon Chang's *Kicking Away the Ladder*
David Brion Davis's *The Problem of Slavery in the Age of Revolution*
Milton Friedman's *The Role of Monetary Policy*
Milton Friedman's *Capitalism and Freedom*
David Graeber's *Debt: the First 5000 Years*
Friedrich Hayek's *The Road to Serfdom*
Karen Ho's *Liquidated: An Ethnography of Wall Street*

John Maynard Keynes's *The General Theory of Employment, Interest and Money*
Charles P. Kindleberger's *Manias, Panics and Crashes*
Robert Lucas's *Why Doesn't Capital Flow from Rich to Poor Countries?*
Burton G. Malkiel's *A Random Walk Down Wall Street*
Thomas Robert Malthus's *An Essay on the Principle of Population*
Karl Marx's *Capital*
Thomas Piketty's *Capital in the Twenty-First Century*
Amartya Sen's *Development as Freedom*
Adam Smith's *The Wealth of Nations*
Nassim Nicholas Taleb's *The Black Swan: The Impact of the Highly Improbable*
Amos Tversky's & Daniel Kahneman's *Judgment under Uncertainty: Heuristics and Biases*
Mahbub Ul Haq's *Reflections on Human Development*
Max Weber's *The Protestant Ethic and the Spirit of Capitalism*

FEMINISM AND GENDER STUDIES

Judith Butler's *Gender Trouble*
Simone De Beauvoir's *The Second Sex*
Michel Foucault's *History of Sexuality*
Betty Friedan's *The Feminine Mystique*
Saba Mahmood's *The Politics of Piety: The Islamic Revival and the Feminist Subjec*t
Joan Wallach Scott's *Gender and the Politics of History*
Mary Wollstonecraft's *A Vindication of the Rights of Women*
Virginia Woolf's *A Room of One's Own*

GEOGRAPHY

The Brundtland Report's *Our Common Future*
Rachel Carson's *Silent Spring*
Charles Darwin's *On the Origin of Species*
James Ferguson's *The Anti-Politics Machine*
Jane Jacobs's *The Death and Life of Great American Cities*
James Lovelock's *Gaia: A New Look at Life on Earth*
Amartya Sen's *Development as Freedom*
Mathis Wackernagel & William Rees's *Our Ecological Footprint*

HISTORY

Janet Abu-Lughod's *Before European Hegemony*
Benedict Anderson's *Imagined Communities*
Bernard Bailyn's *The Ideological Origins of the American Revolution*
Hanna Batatu's *The Old Social Classes And The Revolutionary Movements Of Iraq*
Christopher Browning's *Ordinary Men: Reserve Police Batallion 101 and the Final Solution in Poland*
Edmund Burke's *Reflections on the Revolution in France*
William Cronon's *Nature's Metropolis: Chicago And The Great West*
Alfred W. Crosby's *The Columbian Exchange*
Hamid Dabashi's *Iran: A People Interrupted*
David Brion Davis's *The Problem of Slavery in the Age of Revolution*
Nathalie Zemon Davis's *The Return of Martin Guerre*
Jared Diamond's *Guns, Germs & Steel: the Fate of Human Societies*
Frank Dikotter's *Mao's Great Famine*
John W Dower's *War Without Mercy: Race And Power In The Pacific War*
W. E. B. Du Bois's *The Souls of Black Folk*
Richard J. Evans's *In Defence of History*
Lucien Febvre's *The Problem of Unbelief in the 16th Century*
Sheila Fitzpatrick's *Everyday Stalinism*

Eric Foner's *Reconstruction: America's Unfinished Revolution, 1863-1877*
Michel Foucault's *Discipline and Punish*
Michel Foucault's *History of Sexuality*
Francis Fukuyama's *The End of History and the Last Man*
John Lewis Gaddis's *We Now Know: Rethinking Cold War History*
Ernest Gellner's *Nations and Nationalism*
Eugene Genovese's *Roll, Jordan, Roll: The World the Slaves Made*
Carlo Ginzburg's *The Night Battles*
Daniel Goldhagen's *Hitler's Willing Executioners*
Jack Goldstone's *Revolution and Rebellion in the Early Modern World*
Antonio Gramsci's *The Prison Notebooks*
Alexander Hamilton, John Jay & James Madison's *The Federalist Papers*
Christopher Hill's *The World Turned Upside Down*
Carole Hillenbrand's *The Crusades: Islamic Perspectives*
Thomas Hobbes's *Leviathan*
Eric Hobsbawm's *The Age Of Revolution*
John A. Hobson's *Imperialism: A Study*
Albert Hourani's *History of the Arab Peoples*
Samuel P. Huntington's *The Clash of Civilizations and the Remaking of World Order*
C. L. R. James's *The Black Jacobins*
Tony Judt's *Postwar: A History of Europe Since 1945*
Ernst Kantorowicz's *The King's Two Bodies: A Study in Medieval Political Theology*
Paul Kennedy's *The Rise and Fall of the Great Powers*
Ian Kershaw's *The "Hitler Myth": Image and Reality in the Third Reich*
John Maynard Keynes's *The General Theory of Employment, Interest and Money*
Charles P. Kindleberger's *Manias, Panics and Crashes*
Martin Luther King Jr's *Why We Can't Wait*
Henry Kissinger's *World Order: Reflections on the Character of Nations and the Course of History*
Thomas Kuhn's *The Structure of Scientific Revolutions*
Georges Lefebvre's *The Coming of the French Revolution*
John Locke's *Two Treatises of Government*
Niccolò Machiavelli's *The Prince*
Thomas Robert Malthus's *An Essay on the Principle of Population*
Mahmood Mamdani's *Citizen and Subject: Contemporary Africa And The Legacy Of Late Colonialism*
Karl Marx's *Capital*
Stanley Milgram's *Obedience to Authority*
John Stuart Mill's *On Liberty*
Thomas Paine's *Common Sense*
Thomas Paine's *Rights of Man*
Geoffrey Parker's *Global Crisis: War, Climate Change and Catastrophe in the Seventeenth Century*
Jonathan Riley-Smith's *The First Crusade and the Idea of Crusading*
Jean-Jacques Rousseau's *The Social Contract*
Joan Wallach Scott's *Gender and the Politics of History*
Theda Skocpol's *States and Social Revolutions*
Adam Smith's *The Wealth of Nations*
Timothy Snyder's *Bloodlands: Europe Between Hitler and Stalin*
Sun Tzu's *The Art of War*
Keith Thomas's *Religion and the Decline of Magic*
Thucydides's *The History of the Peloponnesian War*
Frederick Jackson Turner's *The Significance of the Frontier in American History*
Odd Arne Westad's *The Global Cold War: Third World Interventions And The Making Of Our Times*

LITERATURE

Chinua Achebe's *An Image of Africa: Racism in Conrad's Heart of Darkness*
Roland Barthes's *Mythologies*
Homi K. Bhabha's *The Location of Culture*
Judith Butler's *Gender Trouble*
Simone De Beauvoir's *The Second Sex*
Ferdinand De Saussure's *Course in General Linguistics*
T. S. Eliot's *The Sacred Wood: Essays on Poetry and Criticism*
Zora Neale Huston's *Characteristics of Negro Expression*
Toni Morrison's *Playing in the Dark: Whiteness in the American Literary Imagination*
Edward Said's *Orientalism*
Gayatri Chakravorty Spivak's *Can the Subaltern Speak?*
Mary Wollstonecraft's *A Vindication of the Rights of Women*
Virginia Woolf's *A Room of One's Own*

PHILOSOPHY

Elizabeth Anscombe's *Modern Moral Philosophy*
Hannah Arendt's *The Human Condition*
Aristotle's *Metaphysics*
Aristotle's *Nicomachean Ethics*
Edmund Gettier's *Is Justified True Belief Knowledge?*
Georg Wilhelm Friedrich Hegel's *Phenomenology of Spirit*
David Hume's *Dialogues Concerning Natural Religion*
David Hume's *The Enquiry for Human Understanding*
Immanuel Kant's *Religion within the Boundaries of Mere Reason*
Immanuel Kant's *Critique of Pure Reason*
Søren Kierkegaard's *The Sickness Unto Death*
Søren Kierkegaard's *Fear and Trembling*
C. S. Lewis's *The Abolition of Man*
Alasdair MacIntyre's *After Virtue*
Marcus Aurelius's *Meditations*
Friedrich Nietzsche's *On the Genealogy of Morality*
Friedrich Nietzsche's *Beyond Good and Evil*
Plato's *Republic*
Plato's *Symposium*
Jean-Jacques Rousseau's *The Social Contract*
Gilbert Ryle's *The Concept of Mind*
Baruch Spinoza's *Ethics*
Sun Tzu's *The Art of War*
Ludwig Wittgenstein's *Philosophical Investigations*

POLITICS

Benedict Anderson's *Imagined Communities*
Aristotle's *Politics*
Bernard Bailyn's *The Ideological Origins of the American Revolution*
Edmund Burke's *Reflections on the Revolution in France*
John C. Calhoun's *A Disquisition on Government*
Ha-Joon Chang's *Kicking Away the Ladder*
Hamid Dabashi's *Iran: A People Interrupted*
Hamid Dabashi's *Theology of Discontent: The Ideological Foundation of the Islamic Revolution in Iran*
Robert Dahl's *Democracy and its Critics*
Robert Dahl's *Who Governs?*
David Brion Davis's *The Problem of Slavery in the Age of Revolution*

Alexis De Tocqueville's *Democracy in America*
James Ferguson's *The Anti-Politics Machine*
Frank Dikotter's *Mao's Great Famine*
Sheila Fitzpatrick's *Everyday Stalinism*
Eric Foner's *Reconstruction: America's Unfinished Revolution, 1863-1877*
Milton Friedman's *Capitalism and Freedom*
Francis Fukuyama's *The End of History and the Last Man*
John Lewis Gaddis's *We Now Know: Rethinking Cold War History*
Ernest Gellner's *Nations and Nationalism*
David Graeber's *Debt: the First 5000 Years*
Antonio Gramsci's *The Prison Notebooks*
Alexander Hamilton, John Jay & James Madison's *The Federalist Papers*
Friedrich Hayek's *The Road to Serfdom*
Christopher Hill's *The World Turned Upside Down*
Thomas Hobbes's *Leviathan*
John A. Hobson's *Imperialism: A Study*
Samuel P. Huntington's *The Clash of Civilizations and the Remaking of World Order*
Tony Judt's *Postwar: A History of Europe Since 1945*
David C. Kang's *China Rising: Peace, Power and Order in East Asia*
Paul Kennedy's *The Rise and Fall of Great Powers*
Robert Keohane's *After Hegemony*
Martin Luther King Jr.'s *Why We Can't Wait*
Henry Kissinger's *World Order: Reflections on the Character of Nations and the Course of History*
John Locke's *Two Treatises of Government*
Niccolò Machiavelli's *The Prince*
Thomas Robert Malthus's *An Essay on the Principle of Population*
Mahmood Mamdani's *Citizen and Subject: Contemporary Africa And The Legacy Of
Late Colonialism*
Karl Marx's *Capital*
John Stuart Mill's *On Liberty*
John Stuart Mill's *Utilitarianism*
Hans Morgenthau's *Politics Among Nations*
Thomas Paine's *Common Sense*
Thomas Paine's *Rights of Man*
Thomas Piketty's *Capital in the Twenty-First Century*
Robert D. Putman's *Bowling Alone*
John Rawls's *Theory of Justice*
Jean-Jacques Rousseau's *The Social Contract*
Theda Skocpol's *States and Social Revolutions*
Adam Smith's *The Wealth of Nations*
Sun Tzu's *The Art of War*
Henry David Thoreau's *Civil Disobedience*
Thucydides's *The History of the Peloponnesian War*
Kenneth Waltz's *Theory of International Politics*
Max Weber's *Politics as a Vocation*
Odd Arne Westad's *The Global Cold War: Third World Interventions And The Making Of Our Times*

POSTCOLONIAL STUDIES

Roland Barthes's *Mythologies*
Frantz Fanon's *Black Skin, White Masks*
Homi K. Bhabha's *The Location of Culture*
Gustavo Gutiérrez's *A Theology of Liberation*
Edward Said's *Orientalism*
Gayatri Chakravorty Spivak's *Can the Subaltern Speak?*

PSYCHOLOGY

Gordon Allport's *The Nature of Prejudice*
Alan Baddeley & Graham Hitch's *Aggression: A Social Learning Analysis*
Albert Bandura's *Aggression: A Social Learning Analysis*
Leon Festinger's *A Theory of Cognitive Dissonance*
Sigmund Freud's *The Interpretation of Dreams*
Betty Friedan's *The Feminine Mystique*
Michael R. Gottfredson & Travis Hirschi's *A General Theory of Crime*
Eric Hoffer's *The True Believer: Thoughts on the Nature of Mass Movements*
William James's *Principles of Psychology*
Elizabeth Loftus's *Eyewitness Testimony*
A. H. Maslow's *A Theory of Human Motivation*
Stanley Milgram's *Obedience to Authority*
Steven Pinker's *The Better Angels of Our Nature*
Oliver Sacks's *The Man Who Mistook His Wife For a Hat*
Richard Thaler & Cass Sunstein's *Nudge: Improving Decisions About Health, Wealth and Happiness*
Amos Tversky's *Judgment under Uncertainty: Heuristics and Biases*
Philip Zimbardo's *The Lucifer Effect*

SCIENCE

Rachel Carson's *Silent Spring*
William Cronon's *Nature's Metropolis: Chicago And The Great West*
Alfred W. Crosby's *The Columbian Exchange*
Charles Darwin's *On the Origin of Species*
Richard Dawkin's *The Selfish Gene*
Thomas Kuhn's *The Structure of Scientific Revolutions*
Geoffrey Parker's *Global Crisis: War, Climate Change and Catastrophe in the Seventeenth Century*
Mathis Wackernagel & William Rees's *Our Ecological Footprint*

SOCIOLOGY

Michelle Alexander's *The New Jim Crow: Mass Incarceration in the Age of Colorblindness*
Gordon Allport's *The Nature of Prejudice*
Albert Bandura's *Aggression: A Social Learning Analysis*
Hanna Batatu's *The Old Social Classes And The Revolutionary Movements Of Iraq*
Ha-Joon Chang's *Kicking Away the Ladder*
W. E. B. Du Bois's *The Souls of Black Folk*
Émile Durkheim's *On Suicide*
Frantz Fanon's *Black Skin, White Masks*
Frantz Fanon's *The Wretched of the Earth*
Eric Foner's *Reconstruction: America's Unfinished Revolution, 1863-1877*
Eugene Genovese's *Roll, Jordan, Roll: The World the Slaves Made*
Jack Goldstone's *Revolution and Rebellion in the Early Modern World*
Antonio Gramsci's *The Prison Notebooks*
Richard Herrnstein & Charles A Murray's *The Bell Curve: Intelligence and Class Structure in American Life*
Eric Hoffer's *The True Believer: Thoughts on the Nature of Mass Movements*
Jane Jacobs's *The Death and Life of Great American Cities*
Robert Lucas's *Why Doesn't Capital Flow from Rich to Poor Countries?*
Jay Macleod's *Ain't No Makin' It: Aspirations and Attainment in a Low Income Neighborhood*
Elaine May's *Homeward Bound: American Families in the Cold War Era*
Douglas McGregor's *The Human Side of Enterprise*
C. Wright Mills's *The Sociological Imagination*

Thomas Piketty's *Capital in the Twenty-First Century*
Robert D. Putman's *Bowling Alone*
David Riesman's *The Lonely Crowd: A Study of the Changing American Character*
Edward Said's *Orientalism*
Joan Wallach Scott's *Gender and the Politics of History*
Theda Skocpol's *States and Social Revolutions*
Max Weber's *The Protestant Ethic and the Spirit of Capitalism*

THEOLOGY

Augustine's *Confessions*
Benedict's *Rule of St Benedict*
Gustavo Gutiérrez's *A Theology of Liberation*
Carole Hillenbrand's *The Crusades: Islamic Perspectives*
David Hume's *Dialogues Concerning Natural Religion*
Immanuel Kant's *Religion within the Boundaries of Mere Reason*
Ernst Kantorowicz's *The King's Two Bodies: A Study in Medieval Political Theology*
Søren Kierkegaard's *The Sickness Unto Death*
C. S. Lewis's *The Abolition of Man*
Saba Mahmood's *The Politics of Piety: The Islamic Revival and the Feminist Subject*
Baruch Spinoza's *Ethics*
Keith Thomas's *Religion and the Decline of Magic*

COMING SOON

Chris Argyris's *The Individual and the Organisation*
Seyla Benhabib's *The Rights of Others*
Walter Benjamin's *The Work Of Art in the Age of Mechanical Reproduction*
John Berger's *Ways of Seeing*
Pierre Bourdieu's *Outline of a Theory of Practice*
Mary Douglas's *Purity and Danger*
Roland Dworkin's *Taking Rights Seriously*
James G. March's *Exploration and Exploitation in Organisational Learning*
Ikujiro Nonaka's *A Dynamic Theory of Organizational Knowledge Creation*
Griselda Pollock's *Vision and Difference*
Amartya Sen's *Inequality Re-Examined*
Susan Sontag's *On Photography*
Yasser Tabbaa's *The Transformation of Islamic Art*
Ludwig von Mises's *Theory of Money and Credit*

The Macat Library By Discipline